POWER

FOR
YOUR DAY

D E V O T I O N A L

POWER
FOR
YOUR DAY

D E V O T I O N A L

*45 Days to Finding More Purpose
and Peace in Your Life*

SAMUEL RODRIGUEZ

Chosen

a division of Baker Publishing Group
Minneapolis, Minnesota

© 2022 by Samuel Rodriguez

Published by Chosen Books
11400 Hampshire Avenue South
Minneapolis, Minnesota 55438
www.chosenbooks.com

Chosen Books is a division of
Baker Publishing Group, Grand Rapids, Michigan

Printed in the United States of America

ISBN 978-0-8007-6274-2 (casebound)
ISBN 978-1-4934-3924-9 (ebook)

Library of Congress Control Number: 2022017698

22   23   24   25   26   27   28   7   6   5   4   3   2   1

I dedicate this book to all the "plow-pushers."
To all the mothers and fathers, husbands and wives,
teachers and students, leaders and followers,
and to all those fully committed to preserving
the "mantle" for the next generation.
Let's do one thing together;
let's go change the world!

Introduction

God's power, purpose and peace are available to you every day—but you must be ready to receive them. And that requires being deliberate about your focus.

Perhaps more than ever, our lives are filled with distractions, destructions and detachments consuming our time, energy and attention. From one day to another, we often struggle to focus on what matters most: our relationship with the living God. While we may not be able to control the challenges we face, we can determine how we respond to them.

We always have a choice, and our choice right now is clear: We can give in to our emotions amid overwhelming, tumultuous circumstances, or we can live by faith through the power of God's Spirit. Considering my own struggles and moments of doubt, I believe the only choice forward is by faith. I believe the only source of truth we can trust above and beyond any other is God's Word. So when I looked to it to light our path in this present darkness, I turned to the example I see in two heroes of the faith: Elijah and Elisha.

I have always been inspired by the diligence, dedication and devotion displayed in their lives during one of Israel's darkest historical periods. They lived during one of the most corrupt, violent, immoral times ever, and yet they remained faithful to God and experienced His faithfulness, power and provision in the face of impossible odds.

The essence of their message to us today emerges vividly in their first meeting: "So Elijah went and found Elisha son of Shaphat plowing a field. There were twelve teams of oxen in the field, and Elisha was plowing with the twelfth team. Elijah went over to him and threw his cloak across his shoulders and then walked away" (1 Kings 19:19 NLT).

Simply put, *your plow precedes your mantle.*

Elijah was led by God to find a successor, a younger protégé. The man God chose, Elisha, was not only a hard worker but was actually in the field plowing with a team of oxen when Elijah first laid eyes on him. And while Elijah did not literally push a plow, he endured droughts, famines, fire and floods before coming into the full power of God's mantle on his shoulders. Both men plowed through the trials, tempests and temptations of life before receiving God's prophetic mantle of divine power. Their examples not only speak to us today but also echo into our lives like thunder across the centuries.

Today, it's so easy to lose your spiritual momentum and get distracted from what's truly important. You want to strengthen your faith and live in the power of the Holy Spirit, but so many emotions cripple your progress. This is why you need *Power for Your Day*—a spiritual second wind and a fresh burst of God's power infusing every area of your life!

Power for Your Day is based on my book *Persevere with Power*. Each day's burst of power includes:

Your Daily Power Point—a key principle or lesson of truth you can apply to your own life based on the examples of Elijah and Elisha.

Your Daily Reading—an exploration of the Power Point based on my examination of God's Word and my findings in *Persevere with Power*.

Your Daily Scripture—a thematically related and curated verse or brief passage from God's Word to energize you with the power of spiritual truth.

Your Daily Prayer Starter—a few sentences to lead you into God's presence as you share your heart in prayer with your heavenly Father.

Wherever you are and whatever you're facing, I know the examples of Elijah and Elisha will encourage, challenge and inspire you to move forward into the glorious future God has for you. Each of the 45 days builds on the others, and the goal is for you to grow deeper in your faith as you reflect on your life and live more fully in the abundant life of God's Spirit. My prayer is that you will find hope, joy, peace and power on every page for every day.

If you want to experience the power to persevere in your life, then it's time to move from your plow to your mantle and from your mantle to your double portion.

It's time to live as a co-heir with Christ instead of a distant relative ashamed to show up.

It's time to stop trying on your own and start relying on the Spirit.

It's time to seek God's power and exercise your mantle.

It's time to start living in the fullness of the power of God's Spirit dwelling in you.

It's time to claim what is rightfully yours and surrender what's no longer your concern.

It's time to persevere with power each and every day!

Samuel Rodriguez

DAY

1

Without a doubt, from Genesis to Revelation, the Bible is not a book of perfect people—it is a book of overcomers!

While you may be tempted to view people in the Bible as perfect saints, they are just as flawed as you and me. God's Word, from beginning to end, is not a catalog of sinless, always-obedient, picture-perfect lives, but instead it shares the stories of flawed-but-faithful men and women persevering amid trials and tribulations. They faced overwhelming obstacles, seemingly impossible situations and dangerous dilemmas that forced them to put their trust in God.

Rather than a roll call of saints, the Bible is a book of overcomers. Just consider some of the best-known believers and what they had to overcome. In the Old Testament, Abraham had to overcome the deceit of others as well as his own tendency to deceive. God promised that he would be the father of many nations, and yet into old age, Abraham and his wife, Sarah, had never conceived—until God gave them their son, Isaac—forcing them to overcome their doubts and the limitations of biological logic.

Consider Joseph, Abraham's great-grandson, and all that he overcame: abandonment in the pit, betrayal by his brothers, the lies of his boss's wife and incarceration. Yet Joseph ended up as Pharaoh's right-hand man, overseeing the harvests, storage and allocation of grain—leadership that saved not only the Egyptians but also Joseph's own family and the nation of Israel.

Many generations later, when the Israelites became enslaved in Egypt, Moses overcame his past, his temper and Pharaoh himself to lead God's people through the Red Sea in pursuit of the Promised Land.

Story after story repeats this theme of overcoming—and the New Testament reinforces it as well. Peter overcame his impulsive nature and the cursing of his blessing. Mary Magdalene overcame her past mistakes and residual reputation. The apostle Paul overcame angry mobs, jail time, earthquakes, shipwrecks and snakebites. And Jesus, the Son of God and our wondrous Savior, overcame darkness, death and defeat—in other words, *everything*!

So follow the example of the overcomers before you and refuse to give up the fight. Don't allow your circumstances to determine the direction of your life. Your battle may not be over, and you may feel weary from the struggle, but God's power in you through the Holy Spirit will always prevail. When you have the Spirit in your life, you no longer depend on your own abilities and limited resources—because you have the unlimited, infinite and eternal power of the living God inside you!

Once you live in the Spirit, you are never the same.

> ## In Christ, by Christ, through Christ and for Christ, you are an overcomer!

For everyone born of God overcomes the world. This is the victory that has overcome the world, even our faith. Who is it that overcomes the world? Only the one who believes that Jesus is the Son of God.

1 John 5:4–5

Lord, thank You for bringing me this far and never giving up on me. Empower me today to do all that You want me to do. Help me to remember that I'm an overcomer because Your Spirit dwells in me. Amen.

DAY

2

We can give in to our emotions amid overwhelming,
tumultuous circumstances, or we can live by
faith through the power of the living God.

Each day, you encounter triggers that threaten to stir up a variety of overwhelming emotions. These catalysts for calamity might pull you back into the past, tempting you to feel trapped by old mistakes, mishaps and missteps. You may even start to believe the enemy's lies that you will never experience joy or peace again. Grief from an accumulation of losses—loved ones, relationships, homes, health, jobs—may swallow your energy and pull you under. Anxiety fueled by past trauma might gnaw away at your perceptions and expectations so that worrying becomes second nature. Fighting depression can take whatever strength remains, which seems like less and less every day.

Current events and cultural shifts may also be keeping you on edge, wounding your heart and worrying your mind with political factions, systemic racism and deteriorating civility. In the clutches of such strong riptide emotions, you might be numbing your pain, both past and present, by relying on old habits and the false comfort of addictive substances.

As you wrestle with the daily assault of aberrant attitudes and belligerent behavior around you, it is no wonder you lack peace and sense hope slipping away. The toll of such unrelenting, stressful emotions leads to chronic discomfort, distortion and disease. Such burdens can, in fact, crush you unless you make a choice and hold fast to your faith.

And your choice is clear today. You can give in to your emotions amid overwhelming, tumultuous circumstances, or you can walk by faith through the power of the living God. While everyone struggles at times and experiences moments of doubt, the only way forward is to trust the Lord and rely on His Word. Throughout the pages of Scripture, you will find eternal truth to be trusted and applied to your daily decisions.

You will also find heroes of the faith there to inspire you. Each man and woman of God in the Bible experienced most if not all of the same feelings you encounter. They overcame the barriers, both external and internal, blocking their paths and attempting to derail their faith. No matter how they felt in the midst of harsh circumstances, they trusted God for a bigger picture. This is the divine coping mechanism we see exemplified by the life of Jesus. He felt the entire spectrum of human emotions—love, hate, anger and disappointment, to name a few—without allowing those feelings to obscure His knowledge of truth and His relationship with His Father.

Following Christ's example, you can do the same.

> You cannot control what you feel, but you can choose how you respond to your feelings.

For we do not have a high priest who is unable to empathize with our weaknesses, but we have one who has been tempted in every way, just as we are—yet he did not sin.

Hebrews 4:15

· · · · ·

Dear God, give me strength today through the power of the Holy Spirit to rise above my emotions and walk by faith instead. Remind me that I always have a choice, no matter what feelings may arise. Thank You for showing me the way. Amen.

DAY
3

The examples of Elijah and Elisha demonstrate a fundamental principle of God's Kingdom: If you want to wear the mantle of divine favor, you must push your plow with diligence.

I f you're craving hope amid dark times, you might be surprised by the way two Old Testament prophets, Elijah and his successor, Elisha, inspire present-day diligence, dedication and devotion. During one of Israel's bleakest historical periods, a violent and immoral time of rebellion and idol worship, Elijah and Elisha remained faithful to God and experienced divine protection, power and provision in the face of impossible odds.

Their examples demonstrate a fundamental principle of God's Kingdom: to be diligent with the resources and responsibilities entrusted to you before expecting to be blessed with more. This truth resonates throughout the Bible and emerges clearly in at least two of the parables Jesus told to His followers. In the parable of the shrewd manager (Luke 16), the master gave notice to his wasteful manager that he was about to lose his job due to mismanagement. The manager, aware that he had no abilities or talents to earn a living any other way, decided that he would prepare for his impending unemployment by reducing the debts owed by the various vendors in his master's household. By doing them favors now, the manager hoped they would return in kind later when he had no other resources.

The parable of the talents echoes a similar theme, although with a twist. When the master prepares for an extended absence by delegating to his three servants, he expects them not only to keep safe the wealth entrusted but to invest it and return a profit. Upon returning, the master finds that two of his faithful servants have done just that, so he tells them: "You have been faithful with a few things; I will put you in charge of many things" (Matthew 25:21). The third, however, has buried the resources he was given, claiming to be motivated by fear of the master's displeasure. Ironically, that's exactly what the third servant gets for squandering what the master had entrusted to him.

This same emphasis on acting responsibly and diligently in order to make the most of one's resources emerges in the first meeting between Elijah and Elisha. After enduring a chain of dramatic circumstances that left him emotionally and physically exhausted, Elijah struggled to push through his fear and anxiety and reclaim his purpose. So, God met Elijah, hiding in a cave on Mount Horeb, and reignited the prophet's purpose with the pursuit of a protégé. "So Elijah went and found Elisha son of Shaphat plowing a field. There were twelve teams of oxen in the field, and Elisha was plowing with the twelfth team. Elijah went over to him and threw his cloak across his shoulders and then walked away" (1 Kings 19:19 NLT).

> **Today, push your present plow so that you will be ready for your future mantle.**

Whoever can be trusted with very little can also be trusted with much, and whoever is dishonest with very little will also be dishonest with much.

Luke 16:10

. . . . .

Father, help me to be shrewd and savvy with the resources and responsibilities entrusted to me. I want to please You today in everything I do. May I do my best so that Your glory may be magnified. Amen.

DAY
4

Just as Elisha's plow prepared him to wear God's mantle, when we faithfully carry out the roles and responsibilities God assigns us, then He gives us more—more power, more provision, more passion—to meet the next challenges we're called to face.

Elijah was a man with a mantle, a message and a mission. Although he was God's prophet, Elijah didn't enjoy an easy life of comfort and convenience. He was called to preach a message of repentance to the people of Israel, including its wicked King Ahab and Queen Jezebel, who were worshiping idols. Elijah met resistance at every turn, even after winning a spiritual showdown where he demonstrated God's immense power over the impotence of idols. Running for his life from the vindictive sovereigns, Elijah became discouraged and depressed until God met him and gave him a new mission: to go find his successor, Elisha, and mentor him as God's prophet.

Renewed by God's loving care and confidence in him, Elijah went in search of the younger man who was to become his protégé and found him leading a team of oxen and plowing a field (see 1 Kings 19:19–21). Elijah then placed his mantle on Elisha, indicating that it was time for Elisha to leave his plow behind and take on the new role and responsibilities for which God had anointed him. It's no coincidence that Elisha had been farming the land prior to receiving his mantle.

Farming requires hard work, dedication, vigilance, patience and perseverance—all traits that would serve Elisha well in his new role as prophet. As a farmer, Elisha invested his labor in plowing fields, planting seeds, protecting the crop and harvesting the fruit of his investment. He had no idea God was preparing him for a much greater role and more power. Elijah simply did his best to fulfill the responsibilities required to steward the land and produce a harvest.

God used these life skills to build Elisha's character in anticipation of the role God had for him. Elisha's plow prepared him to wear God's mantle and wield the power and responsibility that came with its wearing. The same cause-and-effect sequence of spiritual growth and unlimited holy power continues to operate today. When we faithfully carry out the roles and responsibilities, the duties and directives, God assigns us, then He gives us more—more power, more provision, more passion—to meet the next challenges we're called to face.

Although we usually don't like trials and challenges, James tells us, "Consider it pure joy, my brothers and sisters, whenever you face trials of many kinds, because you know that the testing of your faith produces perseverance" (James 1:2–3). When you know God is training, equipping and preparing you for greater service, then you can endure painful moments and tough times because you know that they serve His perfect purpose. Your mantle is waiting on you, so remain patient while pushing your plow!

You have been entrusted by God to do great things—now and in the future!

Each of you should use whatever gift you have received to serve others, as faithful stewards of God's grace in its various forms.

1 Peter 4:10

. . . . . .

Lord, give me strength and discernment to be a good steward of all the gifts You have entrusted to me. Give me patience to learn and grow where I am now so that I will be ready for more responsibility when it's time to trade my plow for Your mantle. Amen.

DAY 5

Hard times may leave us in darkness, but they can never separate us from the Light—pathetic times last for a while, but God's prophetic power always triumphs!

While the challenges you face today may seem urgent and unexpected, remember that Elijah and Elisha faced similar forces, embodied by King Ahab and Queen Jezebel, thousands of years ago. These two prophets endured cultural shifts toward immorality, idolatry and individuality that threatened their faith and endangered their lives. Then and now, social forces with access and authority urge us to sacrifice God's truth on the altar of acceptance and expediency. These forces try to tell us what to believe and how to act, coercing us into conforming to their own idolatrous agendas rather than obeying the Word of God.

This intense pressure results from political leaders like Ahab doing whatever is expedient for their own power and profit, pretending to care about their constituents, but intent on exploiting them. They are the social media celebrities and style icons, seducing followers to imitate them without any limits to their language, behavior and morality. They are the corporate executives and media moguls driven by greed and worshiping mammon rather than the truth of the living God.

Modern Jezebels want to construct counterfeit temples and to legitimize bogus institutions that will marginalize noble, God-honoring oracles of righteousness and justice. They are the entertainers offering their self-aggrandizing authority and the advertisers selling self-delusion and vanity. They construct their idolatrous altars and try to drown out the cries of the persecuted, the impoverished, the wounded and those in need.

When we hear the latest news or scroll to our favorite sites, we're often disheartened by the pervasive darkness shrouding our world. Individual trials and suffering become compounded by despair resulting from the pathetic decline of truth in our world today. As followers of Jesus, however, we must never allow such darkness to obscure our vision or diminish our hope.

No matter how discouraged you may feel or how bleak things look, you must remember that nothing can separate you from the power, purpose and peace of the almighty living God. Injustice and prejudice may seem to triumph momentarily, but they will never prevail. The apostle Paul reminds us, "Who shall separate us from the love of Christ? Shall trouble or hardship or persecution or famine or nakedness or danger or sword? . . . No, in all these things we are more than conquerors through him who loved us" (Romans 8:35, 37).

No matter how dark your night, God's morning always comes.

No matter how downcast you may feel, God's presence is always with you.

No matter how desperate your circumstances, God's power always prevails.

Remember that nothing you face today can separate you from the prophetic power of God!

You are the light of the world. . . . Let your light shine before others, that they may see your good deeds and glorify your Father in heaven.

Matthew 5:14, 16

· · · · ·

Dear God, thank You for the peace that passes understanding in my heart today. Remind me that the cultural darkness around me can never quench Your light in my life. Amen.

DAY 6

Pushing your plow prepares you for wearing the mantle God has for you. Don't confuse what you're going *through* with where you're going *to*!

Pathetic times only serve to showcase God's prophetic power.

Despite the repeated disobedience and frequent idolatry of the people of Israel, God didn't abandon them, but He sent prophets, including Elijah and Elisha, with His message of repentance and His power to conquer adversity. While Ahab and Jezebel blatantly worshiped pagan gods and practiced rituals, they only created an opportunity for God to reveal His prophetic power through His people. What they intended for their own glory, greed and pleasure, God used as a showcase to spotlight His character, His love and His mercy.

If Elijah and Elisha had given up and stopped trusting God, then they would have missed out. If they had not persevered with pushing their respective plows, one metaphorical and the other literal, then they would have missed the mantle of blessing God had for them.

You face the same opportunity today. You can be part of what God is doing, or you can sink in the cultural muck trying to pull you under. You can thrash and splash as the relentless currents of unexpected circumstances overwhelm you, or you can grab the lifeline of prophetic power God extends to those who trust Him. You cannot control all that happens to you and around you, but you always have a choice about how to respond.

No matter what you're facing right now, your battle may not be over, but it's already been won! God will never give up on you and will instead anoint you with holy antibodies to overcome the powers of darkness and the infection of sin in your life. So no matter how bleak your circumstances, God's power in you will prevail. Nothing is finished until God declares it finished!

If you're willing to push your plow spiritually, then you can know that God's mantle is waiting for you. And when God's mantle rests on your shoulders, then nothing and no one can stop you! When you have the Spirit of God dwelling in you, you never have to fear pathetic times again. As followers of Jesus who have accepted the gift of salvation through His sacrifice on the cross, we are assured, "But you have received the Holy Spirit, and he lives within you" (1 John 2:27 NLT). You may face trials and tribulations or endure storms and setbacks, but you will never be defeated permanently. You might experience discomfort, distress or debilitation, but your joy and peace will not cease.

> **If you live in the power of the Holy Spirit, nothing can defeat you today!**

And hope does not put us to shame, because God's love has been poured out into our hearts through the Holy Spirit, who has been given to us.

Romans 5:5

. . . . .

Father, I thank You and praise You for the gift of Your Holy Spirit dwelling in me. May I be mindful that where I am today is not where You are leading me tomorrow. Amen.

DAY

7

People who love and serve God in the power of
the Holy Spirit through the sacrifice of Jesus Christ
work to discover their God-given purpose.

God notices how hard you're working and how patiently you're persevering. And He is using your devotion, dedication and diligence to prepare you for greater mantles of promotion in your future. No matter how frustrating, annoying or pointless your present responsibilities and duties may seem, trust God, and do your best to work for His approval and no one else's.

Such pushers of the plow know that they persevere not only to receive the mantle of promotion awaiting them but also to reveal God's power in their lives. When we obediently and diligently serve without putting the focus on our own abilities, we let others glimpse the Lord working through us. We honor God by keeping our commitment to push our plow the same way we try to live our lives: for His glory. "So, whether you eat or drink, or whatever you do, do all to the glory of God" (1 Corinthians 10:31 ESV).

Plowing without grumbling or complaining builds character, strengthens faith and exercises patience. Such practitioners serve God despite their fluctuating feelings and ongoing frustrations, regardless of circumstances and crises. They persevere when others turn back, give up, abandon their plows and run away. They may not be the most talented, most educated, most experienced or even the strongest. But they are the most faithful, loyal, determined and stubborn.

Rather than being discouraged by the vast fields to be plowed before seeds sprout and fruit is harvested, these individuals start at the beginning of each new row and simply push their plows. Step by step, inch by inch, furrow by furrow, they upturn the hard ground to fulfill their dreams. They keep going despite all obstacles blocking the path to progress. These servants of the Lord steward all that He has entrusted to them and push their plows until their mantle arrives.

The kind of plow pushing that leads to mantles of promotion can only be motivated by love, gratitude and trust in the living and almighty God. The apostle Paul makes it clear that giving God all areas of our lives is an act of worship: "Therefore, I urge you, brothers and sisters, in view of God's mercy, to offer your bodies as a living sacrifice, holy and pleasing to God—this is your true and proper worship" (Romans 12:1). We push our plows as a sacrifice to more fully honor the Lord and all He has done, is doing and will do for us.

> **Today, I will push my plow for God's glory and celebrate how He is preparing me for more.**

Whatever you do, work heartily, as for the Lord and not for men, knowing that from the Lord you will receive the inheritance as your reward. You are serving the Lord Christ.

Colossians 3:23–24 ESV

. . . . .

Lord, I devote myself to serving You today in all that I do. May others see Your love in my attitude and manner. Give me patience and strength to focus on the tasks before me even as I anticipate the greater role ahead of me. Amen.

DAY 8

When we obediently, humbly and diligently serve
without putting the focus on our own abilities, we
let others glimpse the Lord working through us.

God seems to choose people for daunting, if not humanly impossible, tasks based on willingness and faith, not talent or experience. The Bible is filled with examples. From Abraham to Jacob, Ruth to Rahab, and Gideon to Esther, each one was willing to serve, to push their plow, despite what they perceived to be their own inadequacies, insecurities and instabilities. God used their willingness to trust Him to reveal His power.

Elijah and Elisha illustrate this same kind of humility and holy trust in the face of overwhelming obstacles. Elijah pushed his plow by persevering through trials every bit as hard and rocky as the fields Elisha plowed. Even when the older prophet reached one of the lowest points in his life, he encountered God and received a fresh sense of purpose from the divine mission he was given—to find Elisha.

When he finally found his new apprentice, Elijah didn't find Elisha basking in the lap of luxury or complaining about the work required. Instead, Elijah found Elisha literally pushing his plow. History tells us that most likely Elisha would wake by dawn every morning, harness the oxen, push the plow, break the ground and sow the seed. There was nothing glamorous or noble about such humble, backbreaking efforts.

Plowing fields implies repetition in uniformed rows that follow a consistent pattern. There's a rhythm and fluidity required to push through hard, rocky terrain or to navigate through soft, muddy ground. Plowing was tedious, strenuous work undertaken by those dedicated to the necessity of providing food not only for their own survival but also to sustain their families, tribes and communities.

In Elisha's day, plowing required mastery and control over beasts of burden, likely donkeys or, as Scripture indicates in this case, oxen. The sheer physicality of plowing required total body strength. Without a doubt, Elisha exerted his shoulders and upper body to hold and guide the plow handles while he maintained balance, control and speed with his torso, thighs, legs and feet. The job required focus as well to keep rows straight and plow animals pulling in tandem.

Upon seeing the straining, sweating figure guiding a team of oxen to plow straight, Elijah's response speaks volumes: Without hesitation he drapes his mantle over Elisha's shoulders. This action of anointing symbolizes several transactions taking place. There is a generational passing of the torch from one servant-leader to another. There's also a kind of anointing from God's present prophet to the one whom the Lord has chosen to succeed Elijah. A bond of collaboration is formed and embraced to do together what neither could do alone.

How do you want others to see your work when it's time to don your mantle?

Humble yourselves, therefore, under God's mighty hand, that he may lift you up in due time. Cast all your anxiety on him because he cares for you.

1 Peter 5:6–7

* * * * *

Dear God, empower me to labor to the best of my ability with humility and patience so that others may see You reflected in my efforts. Remind me that everything I face now strengthens me for the mantle ahead. Amen.

DAY
9

You must not linger behind your plow when God
reveals it's time to assume your mantle.

When Elijah's mantle falls on Elisha, there's an invitation to a new season, a higher level, the next chapter. This invitation might also be interpreted as a kind of reward or recognition—not for plowing the longest time or the straightest rows, but for Elisha's willingness to do the hard work God had placed before him without complaint or resentment. Many people desire the mantle without ever pushing the plow. But they fail to realize that metaphorically and prophetically speaking, the mantle—a symbol of God's assignment, anointing and authority—only descends on those who faithfully push their plows.

You may be tempted to grow impatient and abandon the tasks involved with pushing your present plow. Perhaps you compare yourself to others who seem to have their mantles handed to them without the kind of efforts you continue to invest. Keep in mind that modern technology and social media are not the measuring sticks for the plow pushing you have been called to do. Anyone who becomes accustomed to instant gratification will likely bristle when forced to work without a clear sense of when and how their efforts will be rewarded.

If you're struggling to steady your plow and persevere, remember that most people have times when they struggle to remain faithful. When you encounter trials and temptations, such challenging circumstances often affect both the work you're called to do and your attitude toward doing it. But you must not despair or allow weariness to take its toll.

Wherever you find yourself right now, remember that you must push the plow of perseverance in order to wear the mantle of greater responsibility. And there is a seasonal, sequential order to this progression. You must push the plow before you move on to carry the mantle. Otherwise, you may find yourself unprepared, ill-equipped or relying on your own power instead of God's. The mantle will not fit you or provide you with the covering you need to accomplish what you're called to do.

Also, you must not linger behind your plow when God reveals it is time to assume your mantle. You may be tempted to remain in the safety of the familiar rather than let go of the plow handles so that God can give you something new to hold. But you must trust His timing to wear His mantle.

Do not get stuck behind a plow.

Do not get stuck behind past failures.

And do not get stuck behind past successes.

Like a big fish in a little pond, you may enjoy the recognition from others or the admiration they show for the work you're doing. Pushing your plow, you can demonstrate and showcase your talents, abilities and strengths. But never allow your plow to define you.

Remember, God has much more for you than you can see from behind your present plow!

Let us not become weary in doing good, for at the proper time we will reap a harvest if we do not give up.

Galatians 6:9

. . . . .

Heavenly Father, I trust that what I'm doing now prepares me for Your future. Give me stamina and peace so that I may persevere until the time when Your mantle falls on my shoulders. Amen.

DAY
10

Draw strength from the knowledge that God
values your willingness to push your plow and
persevere toward His mantle ahead.

When you've been pushing your plow for a long time, it's natural to grow weary. You keep doing the same things day after day, and even though others depend on you, they may not show their support or appreciation. You may begin to feel overlooked and taken for granted—or worse, used and exploited. You may be juggling multiple responsibilities and feeling pulled from one plow to another.

Gradually, the weight of your plow becomes heavier and overwhelming. Your body rebels against the schedule you keep, tired and exhausted, which can leave you vulnerable to illness and injury. You persevere but begin to lose perspective, allowing emotions of anger, resentment, frustration, loneliness and insignificance to overwhelm you. Still, you get up every day and go to your plow, doing your best to put your feelings aside in order to keep your commitment. Soon, you probably slip into depression and feel stuck in place, on a treadmill of plowing, plowing, plowing with no end in sight.

If this describes your experience as a plow-pusher, then take a moment to catch your breath. Remember that Jesus told His followers, "Take my yoke upon you and learn from me, for I am gentle and humble in heart, and you will find rest for your souls. For my yoke is easy and my burden is light" (Matthew 11:29–30). While pushing your plow may never seem as easy or light as you would like, Jesus provides the key to getting a second wind as you follow His example and rest in the spiritual peace of the Holy Spirit.

Also, keep in mind that if your plow seems too heavy or feels stuck in place, then you may be pushing the wrong plow. Sometimes you may be doing something you were once called to do long after God has called you to move on. Whether out of fear or doubt or simply by not paying attention to the whisper of the Spirit, you may be suffering because you're holding your plow even when your mantle is ready.

No matter how you feel or who overlooks the ground where you plow, you must know that your heavenly Father sees you and values you. Your Creator designed you for a special and specific purpose, so even if you feel ready for your mantle before it's given, take heart and remain patient. God hasn't forgotten you and will never abandon you. Soon, you will be carrying the mantle of new challenges, new goals, new resources. Take heart and prepare for a holy deposit of God's grace and power that will enable you to magnify the name of Jesus like never before.

Rest in the power of the Holy Spirit today as you push your plow with patience!

Wait for the LORD; be strong and take heart and wait for the LORD.

Psalm 27:14

. . . . .

Lord, I grow weary at times and need Your strength to carry me through the day. Remind me that Your power is in me even as I struggle to push my plow and wait patiently. Thank You that I can rest in You and experience Your peace. Amen.

DAY
11

Plow with patience and persistence as you wait for
God's mantle of promotion. During times of drought,
God miraculously provides for all your needs!

During times of drought, you may struggle to believe that the rain will come. When bills are due and accounts are low, you may wonder how you will ever manage to keep going. When your body aches, you may be afraid to hope that you will experience complete healing. When you battle depression and anxiety, you may feel powerless to break free and enjoy your life again. If you are seeking God and pushing your plow, however, then you can rest assured that He remains faithful and provides for the needs of those who serve Him.

As evidenced by Elijah's experience, God knows your needs and never fails to surprise you with His provision. During a severe drought lasting for years, the Lord told His prophet to camp east of the Jordan River, where Elijah would receive sustenance. Sure enough, once there, "The ravens brought him bread and meat in the morning and bread and meat in the evening, and he drank from the brook" (1 Kings 17:6). Talk about a unique delivery service!

When the brook eventually ran dry because of the drought, God directed Elijah to go to Zarephath, where he would meet a widow with provisions. There, the prophet saw a woman gathering sticks for a fire and asked her for a drink of water as well as some bread to eat (1 Kings 17:10–11). She responded, "As surely as the Lord your God lives . . . I don't have any bread—

only a handful of flour in a jar and a little olive oil in a jug. I am gathering a few sticks to take home and make a meal for myself and my son, that we may eat it—and die" (1 Kings 17:12).

Unfazed by her alarming news, Elijah instructed her to prepare bread for him and then for herself and her son. He promised that miraculously, she would not run out of flour or oil before the drought ended. "She went away and did as Elijah had told her. So there was food every day for Elijah and for the woman and her family. For the jar of flour was not used up and the jug of oil did not run dry, in keeping with the word of the LORD spoken by Elijah" (1 Kings 17:15–16).

This woman demonstrated a willingness to trust God and step out in faith, even when she couldn't see beyond that next step. Rather than despair, she pushed her plow by doing what she could. When asked by a stranger for the impossible, she obeyed Elijah's instructions and received God's miracle provision in return!

> **When we patiently persist in our plowing, the Lord's mantle of miracles sustains us!**

Ask and it will be given to you; seek and you will find; knock and the door will be opened to you. For everyone who asks receives; the one who seeks finds; and to the one who knocks, the door will be opened.

Matthew 7:7–8

. . . . .

Heavenly Father, thank You for the many ways You have provided for my needs in the past. As I consider the challenges ahead, remind me of Your faithfulness and generosity in providing for all my needs. Amen.

DAY
12

God's mantle of promotion for your life requires time
to fit you perfectly, but it's more than worth the wait.

You never have to worry about how your mantle of promotion will fit.

God has designed your mantle for you and you alone, including all you bring—talents, gifts, abilities, experiences—so that it covers every area of your life. Your blessings are bespoken, and your garments of praise proclaim God's glory! The King of kings has chosen you to be co-heirs with His Son, Jesus Christ, and to be filled with His Holy Spirit. When you experience the fullness of this supernatural relationship, you're more than willing to plow faithfully and wait patiently for your mantle of promotion.

Perhaps you struggle to believe that God can really use all your past experiences—including mistakes, disappointments, betrayals and painful losses—to craft your tailor-made mantle of prophetic power. But it's true. No matter what you have been through or where you are right now, God will make sure your mantle fits when the time is right.

Just consider all that Elijah had to endure before he ever met his young apprentice. Prior to following God's instructions to find, anoint and mentor Elisha, the prophet Elijah experienced a series of supernatural adventures rivaling any fictional story you can imagine. And along the way, each incident provided more material for the mantle draping the prophet's shoulders, requiring Elijah to trust God, wait on God, be empowered by God and be used by God.

With wicked idolaters Ahab and Jezebel encouraging their subjects to bow before the pagan gods Baal and Asherah, God used Elijah to get their attention. The Lord spoke through His prophet to remind the people of Israel of His divine power and holy authority as the one true God. But with leaders determined to mock God and kill Elijah, the stage was set for a spiritual showdown between Elijah and the prophets of Baal, assembled by the idol-worshiping king and queen.

When Elijah boldly prayed for the Lord to display His power, God dramatically delivered—and humiliated the idolaters in the process. Consequently, Jezebel vowed to kill Elijah, which apparently frightened him so much he ran for his life. Not only that, but Elijah became so distraught over Israel's stubborn refusal to repent and return to God that he declared himself a failure and his efforts in vain.

Even at his lowest point, when Elijah was exhausted and afraid, God met him where he was and lifted him up. Elijah's actions were not in vain but rather they prepared him to persist with his prophecy of truth and to seek out Elisha. Nothing we do is wasted when we trust God to measure our mantle.

Today, trust that God can redeem everything in your past to empower your future!

In him we have redemption through his blood, the forgiveness of sins, in accordance with the riches of God's grace that he lavished on us.

Ephesians 1:7–8

. . . . .

God, help me to let go of regrets about my past and trust that You will use even my worst moments for Your glorious purposes. Grant me peace and hope, Lord, so that I can walk with confidence today, clothed in Your righteousness. Amen.

DAY
13

Trust that the mantle God gives to you will cover
all areas of your life through all seasons.

S ometimes you can't see what God is doing because you're right there in the midst of it.

Even after you receive your mantle and experience more of God's power, you may still be uncertain where God is leading or how He wants to use your unique gifts and abilities. Keep in mind during these times that what you're going through, and how you get there, is just as relevant to your journey as your actual destination.

Elijah's mantle, the same cloak he would soon drape over his anointed apprentice, Elisha, was not simply a cape, a piece of fabric worn for practical reasons. Yes, such a garment served as the prophet's blanket, pillow, tent, shelter, towel, robe and headdress. Beyond these practical benefits, however, Elijah's mantle embodied and represented the prophetic spiritual authority God had bestowed on him. This mantle was on him, literally and spiritually, when the prophet exercised holy authority and unleashed a drought on the wayward nation of Israel and its idolatrous leaders (1 Kings 17:1). This mantle of miraculous power was on Elijah when he hid in the ravine next to the brook where ravens brought him food (1 Kings 17:6).

When the brook dried up, Elijah gathered his mantle and followed God's direction to the widow in Zarephath, whose flour and oil never ran out (see 1 Kings 17:12–16). After the widow's son became ill and died, the prophet's mantle became a prayer shawl as he cried out to the Lord for healing power to restore the boy's life (see 1 Kings 17:20–21). Elijah's mantle also covered him when he called down fire from heaven (see 1 Kings 18:36–38) and then cried out, "Here comes the rain!" (1 Kings 18:41–45). No matter what he encountered, his prophetic mantle of power, patience and provision was all he needed to dress for success!

As Elijah wore his mantle of God's prophetic power and mighty miracles, the prophet knew what you must always remember: The God of the process is the God of the outcome. You must not confuse the temporary with the permanent, the momentary with the eternal. God wants to enlarge your perspective so that you trust Him both in your present circumstances as well as your uncertain future. When the path you expected to unfold suddenly takes a detour or leads to a dead end, you may be tempted to question and doubt God rather than reconsider your expectations. Trust that the mantle God gives to you will cover all areas of your life through all seasons.

Wear your mantle with confidence as you trust God in all circumstances!

"For I know the plans I have for you," declares the LORD, "plans to prosper you and not to harm you, plans to give you hope and a future."

Jeremiah 29:11

· · · · ·

Lord, I don't always understand why I have experienced certain situations and endured specific losses. Nor do I see how You can use my humble abilities to accomplish great things for Your Kingdom. But I know all things are possible with You—even what seems impossible to me. Amen.

DAY
14

When we patiently persevere through pain in our
plowing, the Lord's mantle of miracles sustains us!

When events go sideways and you experience unexpected losses, how do you usually respond? Some would say it's human nature to express anger and doubt at God, and perhaps those emotions are necessary. But even when you feel anxious and afraid, do not lose hope in the God who gives you your mantle of miraculous power.

The widow who stepped out in faith and experienced God's miraculous provision of flour and oil found herself confronted with one of life's most devastating losses—the death of her child. It's unclear how much time had passed, only that "sometime later" the widow's son became ill and grew worse until he died (1 Kings 17:17). Her response reflects the feelings we often experience during such grief: powerlessness, followed by guilt, and concluding with the temptation to blame God. "What do you have against me, man of God?" the widow asked Elijah. "Did you come to remind me of my sin and kill my son?" (1 Kings 17:18).

Apparently, she assumed that if this prophet of God could save her life with a miracle, then presumably he could also take away life with such divine power. Or maybe she thought that after God had saved her life and that of her son through Elijah, they were entitled to a kind of divine protection with anointed immune systems. Either way, this woman's perspective was limited by the constraints of her human understanding caused by losing her son.

Can you relate? When have you suffered while plowing and doubted God's goodness?

We often rush to the same kinds of doubts, questions and fears when times get hard and something unexpected happens. We're going along, pushing our plow and making sure our rows are neat and our seeds get planted. Perhaps we have received our mantle and witnessed amazing power already, which can sometimes cause us to struggle even more when we experience trials or calamity.

As much as God loves us, nowhere in the Bible does He promise to make our lives problem-free. Because He gave us free will, meaning we can rebel against Him, resulting in the state of our fallen world, we're forced to live in the consequences of our sinful, selfish decisions. God is always present in our midst and willing to hear our prayers, but we are called to sacrifice our own designs and desires in order to serve Him. He asks us to trust that He knows best, despite what our senses, minds and hearts may tell us. While we're not free of trials and tribulations, we are free of having to endure them and overcome them in our own power.

Exercise patience during hard times and trust you will once again experience the divine power of promotion that comes with your mantle!

But those who hope in the LORD will renew their strength. They will soar on wings like eagles; they will run and not grow weary, they will walk and not be faint.

Isaiah 40:31

· · · · ·

Almighty God, when I grow weak and feel weary, may I rely on Your strength and power to persist and persevere. Please help me push through all obstacles today, Lord, so that I can grow closer to You and draw nearer to the mantle You want me to wear. Amen.

DAY
15

Your mantle's heavenly origin does not mean you won't experience trials, temptations and tempests, only that God will equip and empower you to push through them.

When trials and temptations come your way, it can be hard to keep your faith intact. Whether it's a financial drought, social injustice, lingering illness or the personal loss of someone you love, such valleys can leave you exhausted and vulnerable. You want to persevere and trust in the Lord, but you fear you don't have the strength to keep going.

But this is when you must pause and realize that what you're experiencing is strengthening you for the promise of prophetic promotion ahead. James encourages us to remember the outcome beyond our present suffering: "Consider it pure joy, my brothers and sisters, whenever you face trials of many kinds, because you know that the testing of your faith produces perseverance. Let perseverance finish its work so that you may be mature and complete, not lacking anything" (James 1:2–4). In fact, Jesus told His followers that not only could they encounter trials, but that they should plan to walk a rocky path if they wanted to follow His example (John 15:18–20).

No matter what you're experiencing, remember you stand on solid ground.

Others' opinions and perceptions of who we are and what we stand for may change. Our circumstances will change, with some things we can change and influence positively and preventatively and others we can't. But with God there are no "shifting shadows" (James 1:17). He is our solid rock, our immovable foundation, our steady anchor when everything else may seem upside down. Even as we press onward and upward, diligently pushing our plows, we can count on God's mantle of power, purpose, protection and prophecy.

During tough times, take hope and draw courage from the example of Elijah. As God's messenger to the disobedient people of Israel, Elijah proclaimed a deadly drought, performed miracles for meals, brought the dead back to life, summoned fire in a competitive supernatural showdown and unleashed life-giving rain from above. Through it all, he trusted God as his power source.

We are called to do the same. Your mantle's heavenly origin does not mean you won't experience trials, temptations and tempests, only that God will equip and empower you to push through them. And with each storm you endure and each obstacle you overcome, your mantle stretches to accommodate the growing strength of your faith.

As you grow stronger in your faith, you will discover that God's mantle is the ultimate security blanket for your soul. Your mantle reminds you of where you've been and where you're going. Woven from your life's experiences, it's stitched by God's loving purpose for your time on this earth. Your mantle is your testimony of God's faithfulness in your life, your trophy of His triumph over all your trials.

Nothing can separate you from the unlimited prophetic power of the living God!

No temptation has overtaken you that is not common to man. God is faithful, and he will not let you be tempted beyond your ability, but with the temptation he will also provide the way of escape, that you may be able to endure it.

1 Corinthians 10:13 ESV

. . . . .

Dear Lord, forgive me for the times I have failed and yielded to temptation. Thank You for Your grace, mercy and forgiveness. Through the sacrifice of Your Son and the gift of the Holy Spirit, I know that I am more than a conqueror. Amen.

DAY
16

When we exercise the mantle of holy confrontation,
we may be viewed as a troublemaker because
the majority wants the status quo.

n our divisive world of political animosity and civil unrest, we often allow the mantle of holy confrontation to fall from our shoulders. Rather than speak up for what is right in the eyes of God, we hold our tongue in order to conform to the consensus of others. Instead of calling out injustice, unrighteousness, immorality and idolatry in the world around us, we're prone to look the other way to avoid rocking the boat.

It's so much easier to go with the flow, back away from the battle and try to look the other way, because there will be a price to pay, consequences to contend with and changes to make. We risk being "unfriended" and "unliked" on social media, being criticized and chastised by opponents who don't even know what and whom we stand for. Now perhaps more than ever, however, the political, social and cultural divisiveness in our nation and our world requires us to stand apart from the majority, to go against the powerful and to confront the privileged.

Whether we are intimidated by a cultural climate of cancellations and criticism or we fear the fallout from standing firm in our faith, we must muster the courage displayed by Elijah when confronting King Ahab. Following God's instructions, the prophet had declared that the rain would not fall, a way of commanding everyone's attention by suffering the consequences of a life-threatening famine. As the famine stretched into its third year, God told Elijah it was time for a more direct confrontation: "Go and present yourself to Ahab, and I will send rain on the land" (1 Kings 18:1).

Elijah obeyed and set off for what he knew would be an unpleasant meeting at best. Sure enough, upon seeing his least-favorite person approaching, Ahab greeted Elijah with, "Is that you, you troubler of Israel?" (1 Kings 18:17). In other words, "What do you want, you big troublemaker?"

Undaunted, Elijah deflected the accusation into a true reflection of the situation: "I have not made trouble for Israel. . . . But you and your father's family have. You have abandoned the LORD's commands and have followed the Baals" (1 Kings 18:18). Basically, "I'm not the problem—you're the problem!"

When we exercise the mantle of holy confrontation, we may also be viewed as a troublemaker, an instigator, a catalyst for change when everyone around us wants the status quo. Our opponents may call us names or try to negatively influence the perceptions of others so that they, too, will align against us. Our adversaries hope that if they convince others that we're the cause of problems, then we can be silenced. But that's when we must dare to start holy trouble!

> **Remember, what heaven starts, hell cannot stop!**

Now all glory to God, who is able, through his mighty power at work within us, to accomplish infinitely more than we might ask or think.

Ephesians 3:20 NLT

* * * * *

Lord, give me the courage of Elijah to take a stand when confronted with evil, injustice and idolatry. Empower me with the strength of Your Spirit and remind me of the truth of Your Word. I will not be afraid of confrontations that need to be made. Amen.

DAY
17

The power of God's truth will always defeat the impotence of idols—those we create and those others try to impose on us.

You might assume idols are a thing of the past, that worshiping false gods instead of the living God is no longer a relevant dilemma. But sadly enough, idolatry is alive and well in the 21st century.

Contemporary idols are probably not called Baal and Asherah, like those chosen by Ahab and Jezebel, but they are idols just the same. Idols today are more likely to be found on our phones, on social media, in the clothes we wear, the cars we drive, the homes in which we live and the money we accumulate. For some people, their idols might be their grown-up toys, like sports cars, boats and ATVs. For others, they find security in their identity as someone who enjoys certain hobbies, collects special treasures or regularly travels to exotic destinations—primarily for posting their acquisitions and adventures online.

There is nothing wrong with any of these pursuits or possessions—only in how you regard them. Because if you rely on money, power and material objects to define you and their acquisition to assure you, then you're guilty of the same practice as Ahab, Jezebel and the wayward people of Israel. Whether we're aware of it or not, we are worshiping idols just as they did.

God is the only One who can give us the ultimate security and absolute certainty we long to know. The Bible assures us, "Jesus Christ is the same yesterday and today and forever" (Hebrews 13:8 ESV). He alone is the "author and finisher of our faith" (Hebrews 12:2 NKJV), our Creator who will finish the good work He has started in our lives (Philippians 1:6). We can pray joyfully and confidently the words of the psalmist:

> If you say, "The LORD is my refuge,"
>   and you make the Most High your dwelling,
> no harm will overtake you,
>   no disaster will come near your tent.
> For he will command his angels concerning you
>   to guard you in all your ways;
> they will lift you up in their hands,
>   so that you will not strike your foot against a stone.
>
> Psalm 91:9–12

When we walk with God and wear His mantle over our lives, we have no need of anything the world offers. No earthly idol compares with the eternal assurance of God's love—in this life and the life to come. So like Elisha, push your plow as you persevere with diligence, and like Elijah, wear your mantle with full authority of your prophetic power through the Spirit of the living God!

> **Only the Lord is worthy of your praise, worship and devotion, not idols. Only God can anoint you with His mantle of prophetic power!**

Do not store up for yourselves treasures on earth, where moths and vermin destroy, and where thieves break in and steal. But store up for yourselves treasures in heaven . . . for where your treasure is, there your heart will be also.

Matthew 6:19–21

· · · · ·

Lord, I love You, and I renounce the false idols in my life and the material possessions I have pursued instead of You at times. Your mantle is the only security blanket I need as I remember You are always with me and Your Spirit lives inside me. Amen.

DAY 18

When God's Spirit empowers you for a holy confrontation,
the results always glorify God and advance His Kingdom!

Wearing your mantle of prophetic power and following the Spirit's guidance, you will find courage for the inevitable holy confrontations in your life. Why are they unavoidable? Because of the friction between good and evil, between heaven and earth, between the Spirit of God and the spirit of the world. Jesus told His followers, "If the world hates you, keep in mind that it hated me first. If you belonged to the world, it would love you as its own. As it is, you do not belong to the world, but I have chosen you out of the world. That is why the world hates you" (John 15:18–19).

When called into a holy confrontation, trust that not only will God empower your victory—He will also advance His Kingdom and display His glory for others to see. We see this outcome in the spiritual showdown Elijah initiated after King Ahab called the prophet a troublemaker. As if to prove his point about the true source of Israel's problems, Elijah gave an ultimatum—to the people of Israel, to their king and queen and to their bogus collection of pagan gods.

Two altars would be built, two sacrificial bulls would be chosen and two prayers would be offered—one by the prophets of Baal and the other by Elijah. Then, whichever sacrifice caught fire would reveal the true and living God (1 Kings 18:21–24). With the competition underway, the 450 prophets of Baal prayed and chanted without success—even when Elijah gave them extra time, from morning until evening (1 Kings 18:27–29). Embarrassed by their idol's lack of response, the prophets and spectators then watched in awe as Elijah proved his point even more emphatically.

When it was Elijah's turn, before praying for God to set the sacrificial bull on fire, the prophet dug a trench around the altar and called for four large jugs of water to be doused in the trench, on the stones of the altar and over the carcass of the bull—not just one time but *three* times (1 Kings 18:33–35). Barely had his prayer left his lips when "the fire of the LORD fell and burned up the sacrifice, the wood, the stones and the soil, and also licked up the water in the trench" (1 Kings 18:38).

Incredibly, not only did the sacrifice ignite, but the rocks, wood, dirt and water burned as well! During the blaze, the people watching proclaimed, "The LORD—he is God!" (1 Kings 18:39).

This holy confrontation, with terms agreed upon by those in attendance, ended as an undeniable victory for the one and only holy God, Lord of heaven and earth!

When faced with holy confrontation, trust the outcome will glorify the God who empowers you!

He determines the number of the stars and calls them each by name. Great is our Lord and mighty in power; his understanding has no limit.

Psalm 147:4–5

. . . . .

Almighty God, I marvel at Your limitless power—the same power You make available to me through Your Spirit inside me. When faced with holy confrontations, give me courage and strength to trust You for all outcomes. May You be glorified in all that I do as I serve You and advance Your holy Kingdom. Amen.

DAY 19

When you're in the midst of holy confrontation,
you will usually feel the heat before you see the
fire. Refining you, God removes ideas, thoughts,
actions, behavior and even relationships that would
impede the fulfillment of His purposes.

As you push your plow, break the ground and sow the seed, you will receive a mantle that will empower you to overcome obstacles and adversaries. Knowing and believing this truth, however, will not prevent you from experiencing the discomfort, pain, frustration and inconvenience of life's battles. In fact, when you're in the midst of holy confrontation, you will usually feel the heat before you see the fire. And that heat is often uncomfortable. Even the fire itself, the very evidence you begged Him to send to show His power, can be terrifying.

But going through trials by fire can also be cause for celebration. God's Word says, "In all this you greatly rejoice, though now for a little while you may have had to suffer grief in all kinds of trials. These have come so that the proven genuineness of your faith—of greater worth than gold, which perishes even though refined by fire—may result in praise, glory and honor when Jesus Christ is revealed" (1 Peter 1:6–7). While the fire does not initially make you dance with joy, it ultimately refines, purifies and sanctifies you. Your faith is strengthened because impediments have been burned away.

The fire season is the season in your life when God removes ideas, thoughts, actions, behavior, relationships and even people from your life that in the future would impede the fulfillment of *His* purpose in, with and through you. Going through the fire, you realize your priorities are anchored in Christ Jesus by faith. You emerge stronger, more courageous and more willing to trust God as you move forward.

With the mantle of God fueling his faith, Elijah entered the fire of holy confrontation with the king of Israel. Elijah knew that when God's reputation is on the line, silence is not an option. The mantle of holy confrontation speaks to the truth of only one true God—because when we go through the fire, not only are we refined, but God is revealed and glorified.

As followers of Jesus, we endure the fire by recognizing truth and demonstrating our love in action. Our example must reflect God's love for all people even as it recognizes the travesty, trials and tragedy they may have endured. We issue our call for change not from a political center, but from the prophetic center where righteousness and justice, grace and truth meet in order to bring peace to all human beings made equally in the image of God.

> **As you walk through the fire today, remember what comes next—showers of blessings!**

Praise our God, all peoples, let the sound of his praise be heard; he has preserved our lives and kept our feet from slipping. For you, God, tested us; you refined us like silver.

Psalm 66:8–10

* * * * *

Heavenly Father, when I go through trials by fire, help me to remember that You are still at work, refining my faith and purifying my heart. Thank You for loving me enough to remove all obstacles that could prevent me from wearing Your mantle of prophetic power. Amen.

DAY
20

No matter how powerful, faithful, brilliant, beautiful, rich, educated or accomplished you may be, you overcome because God empowers you with His authority!

lthough they often last longer than you prefer, the droughts end and the fire smolders until the skies open and rain falls. The trials may test your patience as the fires refine your faith, but your hope will be rewarded when clouds burst with heavenly rain. Through the plow pushing and drought enduring, the spiritual reckoning and fire summoning, you trust God to see you through.

Now, looking back, you see how He has prepared and equipped you for the blessings and resources now being entrusted to you. The rain represents holy restoration and renewal, a quenching of the thirst and a filling of the hunger experienced during the drought and the fire. In God's Word, He tells us, "And in the proper season I will send the showers they need. There will be showers of blessing" (Ezekiel 34:26). As life-giving streams of living water nourish and hydrate, you realize that God is going to add over here what you lost back there! "The LORD will send rain at the proper time from his rich treasury in the heavens and will bless all the work you do" (Deuteronomy 28:12).

Just like Elijah, you will persevere and wear the Christ-centered, grace-tailored mantle that is only given after you survive the drought, pray down fire and thrive in the rain. After the holy fire consumed everything on Elijah's altar, Elijah told

Ahab, "Go, eat and drink, for there is the sound of a heavy rain" (1 Kings 18:41). While the king acted on the prophet's recommendation, Elijah "climbed to the top of [Mount] Carmel, bent down to the ground and put his face between his knees" (1 Kings 18:42).

After being the conduit of holy confrontation that God used to silence the idolaters, Elijah humbled himself and gave God all the glory. The prophet knew that when you go high, you must bow low! The more you experience God's outpouring of power, grace, peace and abundance, the more praise and thanksgiving should flow out of you.

Yes, you have overcome so much, and you must never forget all that God has done to bring you to the rain. No matter how powerful, faithful, brilliant, beautiful, rich, educated or accomplished you may be, you never reach mountaintops and experience the rain of restoration in your own power. Only by relying on the limitless power of God's Spirit have you reached a point where you can now soak up His goodness.

> **You overcame because God fought for you, protected you, empowered you and elevated you!**

But he said to me, "My grace is sufficient for you, for my power is made perfect in weakness." Therefore I will boast all the more gladly about my weaknesses, so that Christ's power may rest on me.

2 Corinthians 12:9

. . . . .

Dear God, I praise Your holy name and give You thanks for the many blessings You continue to bestow upon me. I'm so grateful for the way You bring me through the trials and fires of life until I can enjoy the rain. Remind me that Your power always sustains me. Amen.

DAY
21

Spiritual momentum allows you to pick up the pace as you trust God more and more. The more you trust God and step out in faith, the stronger your faith in Him will be the next time you're required to take a risk in moving forward.

You may not know how to define momentum scientifically, but you have most likely experienced it many times. Simply put, momentum describes the way you tend to pick up speed and keep going once you're moving forward. You might recognize the phenomenon of momentum in the way you take care of your home, invest in relationships or complete tasks for work.

For example, you might be cleaning your kitchen, fulfilling orders online or tackling items on your to-do list. Soon you realize that the more you do, the more you want to keep going and do all that needs doing. That sense of picking up speed and continuing at that level until you reach your goal is what momentum is all about.

Spiritual momentum works much the same way. The more we trust God and step out in faith, the stronger our faith in Him will be the next time we're required to take a risk in moving forward. The more we experience God's power, purpose and peace in our lives, the more we want to experience it all the time. The more we get to know the love, kindness and mercy of the Lord, the more we want everyone to know Him as their Lord and Savior.

This kind of pure spiritual momentum might keep us moving forward—in our life, our relationships, our work, our ministry—in a straight trajectory at a consistent pace. In our fallen world full of broken people, however, spiritual momentum can be difficult to maintain. The enemy also wants to derail our spiritual pace with temptations and obstacles. Consequently, instead of growing spiritually at the same pace in the same way no matter what happens day after day, we usually mature at different rates depending on several variables.

Ideally, of course, we would maintain our spiritual momentum no matter what our circumstances happened to be—we wouldn't let our disappointments, failures, regrets and emotions influence our spiritual life. But since none of us are perfect like Jesus, the reality is that we all encounter obstacles that affect our momentum.

When obstacles slow your spiritual pace, the key is to keep going, to step out in faith, relying on God as the Source of your power as well as your speed, day by day. Rather than grow discouraged when we stall or must slow down, we trust that God's perfect timing applies to our rate of growth. He prepares us according to His perfect will so that we grow at just the right pace to become more like Jesus.

No matter what obstacles you encounter today, trust God to set your pace!

In their hearts humans plan their course, but the LORD establishes their steps.

Proverbs 16:9

＊　＊　＊　＊　＊

Lord, sometimes I have rushed ahead when I should have waited on You. Other times, I drag my feet and allow distractions to slow me down. Help me to trust You to set the perfect pace on my journey of faith. Amen.

DAY
22

The speed of life rarely accelerates our spiritual momentum—unless we rely on the power of the Holy Spirit. His Spirit is the breath of fresh air that lifts our sails and gives us a second wind.

The speed of life rarely accelerates your spiritual momentum—unless you rely on the power of the Holy Spirit. You know that in this life you will always have problems, that the world will always persecute you for following Jesus and that the enemy will try to sabotage your spiritual progress. But the tangible expressions of these barriers can often stop you in your tracks.

You want to grow in your faith by developing a steady, strong spiritual momentum, but then you lose your job. Or your child gets sick and requires hospitalization. The car breaks down and needs a new transmission. Bills begin snowballing, until you're overwhelmed by an avalanche of debt. You get sick or injure yourself and become discouraged and impatient by the length of recovery. You feel depressed and anxious by so many events beyond your control, causing you to relapse into an old addiction or bad habit, an unhealthy relationship or destructive pattern.

But life's speed bumps need not deter us from experiencing and maintaining our spiritual momentum. Events may slow us down or send us on detours. Circumstances may momentarily pull us away or send us into an emotional tailspin. We may make wrong decisions and suffer consequences we wish we could have avoided. Sometimes we may worry about what is ahead and slow our momentum without even realizing it.

But through everything we experience, God is there with us. His Spirit is the breath of fresh air that lifts our sails and gives us a second wind. The Bible assures us, "The LORD himself goes before you and will be with you; he will never leave you nor forsake you. Do not be afraid; do not be discouraged" (Deuteronomy 31:8). His Son, Jesus, is the Lord for whom we run our race of life. Like the apostle Paul, we run so as to finish our race and complete the task God has set before us (see Acts 20:23–24). Yes, we may stumble, slow down or slack off, but God is always there to help us get back on our feet and hit our spiritual stride again.

Just as we must push our plows and persevere until we receive our mantles of promotion, we must also learn to maintain spiritual momentum if we are to experience the fullness of all God has for us. He wants us to trust Him for all our needs and not be distracted, disrupted or disturbed by the interruptions, obstacles and adversaries in our lives. We are sons and daughters of the King, created in our Creator's holy image, co-heirs with Jesus Christ and immortal beings temporarily in mortal bodies.

> **Today, run the race set before you with purpose, passion and prophetic power!**

Do not be anxious about anything, but in every situation, by prayer and petition, with thanksgiving, present your requests to God. And the peace of God, which transcends all understanding, will guard your hearts and your minds in Christ Jesus.

Philippians 4:6–7

. . . . .

Holy Spirit, thank You for being the breath of fresh air that gives my soul a second wind. When I slow down or stumble and fall, I know that You will lift me up and help me regain my momentum. Guide me today, Lord, so that I'm in sync with Your rhythm. Amen.

DAY
23

When you're going at a fast speed and suddenly hit a wall
or have someone run into you, you're likely going to be
disoriented. But as you get back on your feet and regain
your bearings, you refocus on what you know is true.

Your enemy, the devil, knows that the way to stop you in your spiritual tracks is by tempting, threatening and taunting you. Once he gets a foothold in your life, once he gets inside your head, then he can prevent you from experiencing the abundant life of a joyful purpose for God's Kingdom. Quite predictably, the enemy often attacks us right after a major spiritual victory.

That's certainly what happened to Elijah. After dramatically defeating the prophets of Baal and humiliating Ahab and Jezebel, Elijah must have been exhilarated. But his victory celebration didn't last long because the angry queen threatened to kill him (see 1 Kings 19:2). Rather than scoff or stand up to such bullying, "Elijah was afraid and ran for his life. When he came to Beersheba in Judah, he left his servant there, while he himself went a day's journey into the wilderness. He came to a broom bush, sat down under it and prayed that he might die" (1 Kings 19:3–4).

How could God's prophet spiral and crash into depression so quickly? Despite all Elijah had seen and experienced—the drought, the holy confrontation, the fire and the rain—he allowed his fears to overcome his faith temporarily.

When he allowed fear to enter his heart and Jezebel to get into his head, Elijah went from being the conductor on a heavenly bullet train to being held hostage by his feelings on a roller coaster. How could Elijah's spiritual momentum come to a screeching halt?

The answer likely requires you to consider your own similar experiences.

You can probably look at your life and see some incredible high points when God intervened in amazing, generous, miraculous ways that you still celebrate to this day. You can likely also see moments when you so disappointed yourself by the way you turned away from God that it still stirs up feelings of shame inside you.

These mile markers remind us that our spiritual momentum is often a stop-and-start-again pace, then a blistering speed of constant advancement, then a time of slowdown or stop.

The important thing is to get moving again.

To remember who you really are, who made you, what you're called to do, where you are right now and where you're going for eternity.

When you're going at a fast speed and suddenly hit a wall or have someone run into you, you are likely going to be disoriented. But as you get back on your feet and regain your bearings, you refocus on what you know is true. How can you stay down when the same Spirit that raised Jesus from the dead lives within you?

When you rely on God to sustain you, you always have the power necessary to keep going!

You need to persevere so that when you have done the will of God, you will receive what he has promised.

Hebrews 10:36

· · · · ·

Father, as I seek to wear Your mantle and serve You today, protect me from the enemy and any temptations he throws my way. Allow me to focus my eyes on Jesus so that I will not be distracted or diverted from running my race with divine momentum. Amen.

DAY 24

When you have the mantle of God on your shoulders, nothing can slow you down! He sets the pace for your spiritual momentum so all you must do is keep walking by faith each day, step by step, stride by stride.

n order to maintain your spiritual momentum, you have to determine whom you will serve and whom you're willing to follow. Some people—online, at work, in the neighborhood—want to provoke you merely to get your attention. They comment, criticize and cancel what you say online only so you will engage with them.

They know that a distraction is the first step to a disruption. If they can get you off-kilter so that you lose focus, you will lose sight of your goal. You may forget the story God has given you to share or be tempted to tell it for the approval of others.

But God calls you to tell your story for His glory, not for your own or for anyone else's approval. For God's glory, tell them about the mountaintop moments when you have seen God work in amazing and miraculous ways in your life. Tell them how the Lord has sustained you through the drought and delivered the holy fire to defeat your enemies and refine the impurities in your life.

Tell your story to those willing to listen and acknowledge God's power and presence in your life. If they join you in worshiping Him as the one and only true God, then you have discovered a friend in the body of Christ. That is the only way they or anyone else can have any authority or credibility to speak into your life—if they are walking with God and serving Him as their Lord and Savior.

More often, others without the spiritual authority to influence you will try to tell you what you should and shouldn't do. These may be online influencers, cultural icons, celebrities, actors, singers, performers, superstar athletes, politicians and civic leaders—and, yes, sometimes even others who claim to be believers, pastors and ministry leaders! Jesus warned us about these wolves in sheep's clothing: "Not everyone who says to me, 'Lord, Lord,' will enter the Kingdom of heaven, but only the one who does the will of my Father who is in heaven" (Matthew 7:21).

Enemies know how to engage us, and once we are engaged, then we can be distracted, divided, diverted and derailed from our God-given purpose. Once we're off-track, our own emotions often do much of the work. As we begin letting our imaginations wander, our worst fears come to mind, and we begin to feel powerless, pulling away from God and the power of the Holy Spirit, often without even realizing it. When we move with the mantle of spiritual momentum, however, our enemies cannot stop us!

Don't let anyone or anything stop you from telling your story and testifying to God's greatness!

Therefore, since we are surrounded by such a great cloud of witnesses, let us throw off everything that hinders and the sin that so easily entangles. And let us run with perseverance the race marked out for us, fixing our eyes on Jesus, the pioneer and perfecter of faith.

Hebrews 12:1–2

. . . . .

Lord, I am so grateful for how You have equipped and prepared me to be where I am right now. Wearing Your mantle, I know nothing can stop me from fulfilling my divine destiny and living for Your glory! Amen.

DAY
25

No matter what enemy, obstacle, barrier, impediment, roadblock, speed bump or pothole we hit, God has already gone ahead of us and provided a way forward.

lijah let his fear get the best of him. After all that he had experienced, after all he had seen God do, after all that he had witnessed, Elijah ran away to hide. He let his trust in the Lord slip away and overlooked the truth of God's Word: "Do not be afraid or discouraged, for the LORD will personally go ahead of you. He will be with you; he will neither fail you nor abandon you" (Deuteronomy 31:8).

With the certainty of this promise fueling the engine of our spiritual momentum, we can keep pressing forward no matter who or what tries to stop us! No matter where we go or what we encounter, God has gone before us to pave the way. Even as Elijah ran to Beersheba, where he left his servant behind and then hid alone under the broom tree, God was already there.

Regardless of what lies before you, when you move toward it, God is already there. He paved your path of promotion before you ever took your first step. So, no matter what enemy, obstacle, barrier, impediment, roadblock, speed bump or pothole you hit, God has already gone ahead of you and provided a way forward.

That river in front of you, God has already crossed.

That mountain standing in your way, God has already climbed.

That viper that came out to poison you, God has already shaken off.

That giant mocking and threatening you, God has already knocked down.

That "Jezebel" making threats to destroy you, God has already silenced.

God always goes ahead and prepares the way for you to do greater things.

All you must do is keep moving, keep trusting, keep going!

God's Word confirms, "I tell you the truth, anyone who believes in me will do the same works I have done, and even greater works, because I am going to be with the Father" (John 14:12).

God goes ahead of you.

God is for you and not against you.

So no matter what you're facing, God has already solved it, fixed it, resolved it, removed it, healed it and sealed it! If you're concerned about your children, your family, your marriage, that medical report, your career, your education, that relationship, that circumstance, that wound from the past, that scar of betrayal, that secret keeping you awake at night, that addiction you're still battling, then here is what you must know: *Let not your heart be troubled.*

God knows, and He is ahead of you working on your behalf.

He is preparing the way, clearing the path, fighting the battles, exposing the traps, mining the diamonds, all because He loves you!

Today, step confidently into the road ahead of you, knowing that God has already paved the way.

And I am convinced that nothing can separate us from God's love. Neither death nor life, neither angels nor demons, neither our fears for today nor our worries about tomorrow—not even the powers of hell can separate us from God's love.

Romans 8:38 NLT

. . . . .

Father, I rest in the knowledge that You are always with me and that nothing can come between us. Thank You for going ahead of whatever is ahead on my path and making a way for me to go forward. Empowered by Your Spirit, I will no longer be held back by my fears, doubts and uncertainty! Amen.

DAY
26

We're often waiting for God to answer our prayers, while He is waiting for us to step out in faith! We assume we're waiting on God's timing, when He is waiting on us to trust Him fully.

Often our instructions from God may not make sense to us in the moment, but only after we obediently carry them out to thwart our enemy and advance God's Kingdom. Similarly, God's directive to us may not seem logical or rational to those around us, but only to His followers who have been anointed. But when God is on the move, we must learn to trust in His divine direction.

This was certainly the case with Elijah. In between winning the big sacrificial showdown and panicking about Jezebel's death threat, Elijah experienced more miracles. After more than three years of drought, God told His prophet that the rain He had promised was about to begin. With very little physical evidence to go on, Elijah instructed the king to return home to Jezreel before the heavy rains set in, something that must have seemed unbelievable if not comical at the time.

Based on his complete confidence in God's declaration, Elijah sent his servant to look for rain—not once but *seven* times! "The seventh time the servant reported, 'A cloud as small as a man's hand is rising from the sea'" (1 Kings 18:44). Now, this tiny wisp of cloud doesn't sound like the beginning of a torrential downpour, but that is exactly what it was, and Elijah recognized it. Acting on his prophetic knowledge of this imminent rainstorm, he instructed Ahab to return home.

Elijah's faith in God to do what He said—send rain after a three-year drought—certainly seems remarkable, but there were precedents. Elijah knew he had witnessed firsthand the way the Lord often used just a little to make a lot. The prophet had seen it near the brook of Cherith when the ravens brought just enough food for him each day, not too much and not too little, but just the right amount. He had seen it with the widow he met in Sidon, a woman of faith who was down to her last dab of oil and last sprinkle of flour—but again, just enough to produce bread for herself, her son and her new guest day after day after day. So, when Elijah heard from his servant that a cloud the size of a man's hand had been spotted, the prophet knew this was more than enough for God to start a torrential gale.

And indeed, it was. Because "soon the sky was black with clouds" followed by a "heavy wind [that] brought a terrific rainstorm" (1 Kings 18:45 NLT). From the tiny cloud spotted by a servant to a fearsome front that sent the king scrambling into his chariot to get home, God once again kept His promise according to His perfect will and wisdom. And He was just getting started!

Today, trust God wholeheartedly for what seems impossible by human standards.

"Truly I tell you, if you have faith as small as a mustard seed, you can say to this mountain, 'Move from here to there,' and it will move. Nothing will be impossible for you."

Matthew 17:20

. . . . .

Dear God, remind me of the many miraculous ways You have provided for me and protected me during my life. Mindful of Your limitless power and amazing love, I know I can do what seems impossible. I place my complete trust in You to do what You say You will do. Amen.

DAY 27

Many people trip on their own cloaks after they
receive their mantle of promotion, having failed
to prepare mentally, emotionally and physically to
handle the new gifts God has poured into them.

Once you have your mantle of promotion, you must be prepared to run with it.

After the tiny cloud ignited the rainstorm, Ahab left in his chariot for Jezreel as Elijah had instructed. And then God did something else astonishing: "The power of the LORD came on Elijah and, tucking his cloak into his belt, he ran ahead of Ahab all the way to Jezreel" (1 Kings 18:46). The distance? About *thirty miles*!

No matter how physically fit Elijah might have been, such a feat required divine strength, stamina and support, which the power of the Lord clearly provided. Winning such an extraordinary race, however, also required Elijah's complete cooperation. He knew he couldn't run the race set before him until he tucked his cloak into his belt.

Left untucked, his loose-fitting garment would only get in the way and entangle his legs and feet—like trying to run a marathon in a bathrobe! Obviously, serious runners try to wear as little as possible so there's nothing to impede their speed. The less clothing, the less weight and the less friction.

Elijah's model of obedience and preparation still applies to us today. We are to travel light and run our race of faith with as little baggage as possible. How do we do this?

Elijah tucked his cloak into his belt before putting one foot in front of the other and experiencing a physical momentum to match the spiritual momentum already in motion. The prophet knew better than to start out, even though the Lord had empowered him, without first doing what had to be done to avoid tripping, stumbling and falling.

Many people trip on their own cloaks after they receive their mantle of promotion. They do the hard work of pushing their plows, and then receive the blessings of more resources to steward. Humbled and excited, they often feel both overwhelmed and unstoppable as they begin moving toward the next level the Lord has for them. Then suddenly, they trip and fall, having failed to prepare mentally, emotionally and physically to handle the new gifts God has poured into them.

People trip over their own anointing and wonder why they aren't experiencing the blessings of their mantle of promotion. Rather than stumble when God empowers us to run, we must do our part to receive His miraculous power. We must remain focused and completely reliant on God rather than taking credit for what He has done through us.

Be prepared to receive the miracle God has for you—and don't forget to tuck and run!

Jesus looked at them and said, "With man this is impossible, but not with God; all things are possible with God."

Mark 10:27

. . . . .

Father God, help me pay attention and be prepared for the divine movements of Your Spirit. Like Elijah, I want to be able to tuck and run so I can race at full speed in my journey of faith. I want to do my part so that I can fully receive Your gifts. Amen.

DAY
28

When God empowers us to do the impossible, we must do
our part to get out of the way, just as we see with Elijah.

Sometimes you may be getting in your own way. After receiving your mantle of promotion, you might be tempted to fixate on your new status, increased responsibility and elevated position. You may even feel entitled to enjoy more blessings than you have received with your new mantle. Nonetheless, you must remain humble and continue serving with diligence, devotion and dedication if you want to fulfill your divine destiny.

It's natural to grow impatient and feel confused and disappointed when our expectations aren't met. We have served faithfully and then experienced God's blessing, yet our lives then don't go as expected. We may worry that we've somehow misunderstood or taken a wrong step. We focus on ourselves rather than on our willingness to trust God completely and wholeheartedly—the qualities that have brought us to this point.

When we get in our own way, the Lord patiently waits for us to exhibit the maturity, wherewithal, fortitude and acumen required to manage the gifts He has given us. Spiritual maturity may look different on different people, but Paul said he knew he was maturing in Christ when the things that used to bother him no longer troubled him. He endured beatings, stonings and lashings; shipwrecks, arrests and snakebites—yet Paul declared,

"If I must boast, I will boast of the things that show my weakness" (2 Corinthians 11:30).

The same goal of spiritual maturity applies to you. When the things that used to get on your nerves no longer do, you are maturing. When the people who were once able to stop you from pursuing your destiny with one little word lose their power to hold you back, you are maturing. When the fleshly desires that once led you into sinful situations no longer have the ability to make you fall, you are maturing. When you're able to say no to the temptations you used to give in to, you are maturing.

When you're willing to tuck your mantle, you are truly willing to be used by God. Too often, we allow the positions, ministries, churches, titles, accomplishments and resources provided by God to define us. In our desire to reorient ourselves to the new responsibilities that come with our mantle, we often wear it as a status symbol, a badge of holy honor for others to see, a spiritual fashion accessory displaying our status and stature.

Your mantle of promotion is none of those things. It doesn't afford you a special standing with God—it reflects what is already in place.

> **When God empowers you to do the impossible, make sure you get out of your own way!**

If I have the gift of prophecy and can fathom all mysteries and all knowledge, and if I have a faith that can move mountains, but do not have love, I am nothing.

1 Corinthians 13:2

. . . . .

God, thank You for entrusting me with Your mantle of promotion and all the responsibilities and blessings that come with it. May I remain humble and use Your bounty to serve You by loving others. Amen.

DAY
29

When you wear the mantle of God's promotion in your life, you're stewarding its prophetic authority for those who will follow behind you.

When you wear the mantle of God's promotion in your own life, you too must realize that you're stewarding its prophetic authority for those who will follow behind you. It's not just a matter of what is necessary or comfortable for you in the moment as you complete the mission or run the specific race. It's a stewardship of what God is doing for those who inherit your mantle.

Notice that before running to Jezreel, Elijah tucked his mantle so it would not slow him down—but he did not discard it. While leaving it behind might have temporarily lightened his load, Elijah's mantle wasn't merely a cloak or garment, something that could be discarded, lost or ignored. His mantle was a symbol of prophetic power, a visual and tactile textile testifying to God's presence and power in Elijah's life.

Much later, after Elijah had mentored Elisha, his mantle of prophetic authority represented his legacy to his successor. This transference took place when Elijah was taken up to heaven by a chariot of fire. "It drove between the two men, separating them, and Elijah was carried by a whirlwind into heaven. Elisha saw it and cried out, 'My father! My father! I see the chariots and charioteers of Israel!' And as they disappeared from sight, Elisha tore his clothes in distress" (2 Kings 2:11–12 NLT). Their powerful parting left the younger prophet feeling alone and perhaps abandoned.

Then Elisha found his way forward as he recognized his spiritual inheritance. "Elisha picked up Elijah's cloak, which had fallen when he was taken up. Then Elisha returned to the bank of the Jordan River. He struck the water with Elijah's cloak and cried out, 'Where is the LORD, the God of Elijah?' Then the river divided, and Elisha went across" (2 Kings 2:13–14 NLT).

Elijah protected the mantle representing his anointing for the next generation. He left it behind so that his protégé, Elisha, could pick it up and assume the authority it symbolically carried. So that day years earlier when Elijah tucked his cloak in his belt before running to beat Ahab to Jezreel, he was not only focused on traveling unencumbered—Elijah was protecting his mantle for the next generation.

Don't forget that you're stewarding your mantle's prophetic authority for those who will follow you in your mission. Don't leave your mantle behind as you start your race—you have plowed too hard and waited too long. Instead, tuck it in your belt and protect it for those who will come after you.

> **Safeguard your mantle, because others will inherit its power after you have crossed the finish line.**

Blessed are those who fear the LORD, who find great delight in his commands. Their children will be mighty in the land; the generation of the upright will be blessed.

Psalm 112:1–2

· · · · ·

Dear Father, as I steward Your mantle of promotion, I will protect it for those who come after me. Give me wisdom and courage, Lord, so that my time serving You will make an eternal difference in the lives of others. Amen.

DAY
30

When you run the good race to the full extent of the divine power bequeathed to you, you can leave the results to God.

Even when you've seen the Lord demonstrate unbelievable, amazing, incredible, miraculous displays of His power, provision and purpose in your life, you may still be tempted to make excuses that prevent you from experiencing all He has for you. Even when your anointing has facilitated miracles in the lives of others, you may still balk when the next opportunity occurs. Even when you're dedicated and committed in all areas of your life to serving God, you may still feel weary, shaken and uncertain about His next mission for your life.

One of the biggest excuses when you're up against adversaries that are better equipped, better resourced and better prepared is that it's too late. Or you set yourself up for failure by letting your mantle get in the way. You allow your anointing to be more important than the One who anointed you in the first place.

The late start didn't prevent Elijah from tucking and running.

The length of the course didn't stop Elijah from doing what others had likely never done.

The weather conditions, terrain and lack of running shoes didn't keep Elijah from running the race God empowered him to run.

While Ahab had horsepower, Elijah had an angelic engine!

When God empowers you, it's never too late, no matter how long the course before you extends. The pathetic may start before you, but the prophetic will always win. The darkness may get a head start, but the light will always finish first. Hell may seem to be in the lead, but heaven will always close the gap and win the race every time.

You may think your creditors will win the battle for your financial solvency, but God's power will provide and meet your needs. Cancer may have started first, but your prayers will unleash God's healing so that your health wins the race. You might assume those who have betrayed you at work have won the promotion, but God doesn't play office favorites. He empowers and blesses those who believe in Him and trust Him with every area of their lives.

God has been waiting for you to mature so you can handle the power that comes with His mantle of promotion. You have pushed your plow. You have survived the drought and summoned the fire. You have watched for the rain and felt it falling on your face. Now it's time to tuck in your cloak and run faster!

When God is with you, it doesn't matter if others have horses, chariots, buggies, jalopies, SUVs or BMWs! You will outrun them all with the power of the Almighty.

> **Today, run your race with your mantle tucked and leave the results to God!**

God's strong hand is on you; he'll promote you at the right time. Live carefree before God; he is most careful with you.

1 Peter 5:6–7 MSG

. . . . .

Lord, sometimes I get discouraged and wonder if it's too late or if I'm up to the task of what You have called me to do. In those moments, God, please remind me that Your strength is perfected in my weakness. I will do my part and trust You for the results. Amen.

DAY
31

As you transition from pushing your plow of perseverance to wearing your mantle of promotion, God will lead you to Gilgal before you continue your journey. There, He reminds you that you have been reborn, changed and set apart.

S ome places symbolize the intersection of events, relationships and milestones in ways that transcend latitude and longitude. You might feel a sense of nostalgia in returning to such places, a blend of remembering the past and tracing your journey into the present with this locale as a launching pad or stopover along the way. Such return visits have been a human practice in ways both secular and sacred for hundreds if not thousands of years.

Many such places feature unparalleled beauty or natural distinctions setting them apart, such as a mountain higher than those around it, like Mount McKinley, or the stunning size of the giant redwoods of Northern California and the Pacific Northwest. Other places draw return visitors not because of any natural features, but due to the events that happened there, such as Independence Hall in Philadelphia or Plymouth Rock, Massachusetts. Some mark the spot where battles were fought or tragedies occurred, such as the shores of Normandy, where Allied forces landed on D-Day during World War II, or Auschwitz, where over a million mostly Jewish prisoners were murdered.

Other locales draw return visits as the site of sacred events, heavenly miracles, divine prophecies and revelations. Not long after Jesus' resurrection and ascension into heaven, many of His followers began traveling to Jerusalem, Nazareth, Bethlehem, the Mount of Olives and the Sea of Galilee. They wanted to see the sites where He walked and talked, healed others and revealed Himself as the long-promised Messiah.

As Christianity spread, more and more visitors ventured to Israel, which soon became known as the Holy Land, to see the places where Jesus had spent His time on earth. By medieval times, believers extended their travels when possible to trace the routes of the apostle Paul and other disciples of Christ. Soon the birthplaces, ministry hubs and gravesites of other venerated saints and recognized giants of the faith began attracting visitors as well. Such travelers came to be known as pilgrims, and their annual trips as pilgrimages.

Even before pilgrimages attracted people to such memorable locations, however, the Bible indicates that some sites were designated as sacred by God Himself. Such is the case for Gilgal, a place identified in the Old Testament as memorable for several significant reasons—including a visit by Elijah and Elisha (2 Kings 2:1). While you probably don't call it Gilgal, you probably know a similar place that reminds you of where you used to be and where God is now leading you. A sacred place for leaving your past behind in order to embrace a glorious future!

> **Pause and take in the view of your spiritual journey, thanking God for how far you have come!**

When hard pressed, I cried to the LORD; he brought me into a spacious place. The LORD is with me; I will not be afraid.

Psalm 118:5–6

. . . . .

Dear God, when I consider the path I have walked with You, I marvel at how far You have brought me. Thank You for never abandoning me and for always showing me where to take my next step. I praise Your name for the many places where You have revealed my purpose. Amen.

DAY 32

Every believer has a similar place to Elijah's Gilgal that reminds us of where we used to be and where God is now leading us—a sacred place for leaving our past behind in order to embrace a glorious future.

Prior to being whisked home to heaven by the Lord, Elijah began a journey to visit spiritually significant places, but it was no coincidence that the prophet's farewell tour began with Gilgal (see 2 Kings 2:1). Accompanied by Elisha, Elijah began at Gilgal because when the Israelites crossed the Jordan River on their way to the Promised Land, they established Gilgal as a monumental site to commemorate their crossing. As Joshua led the people of Israel, the Lord miraculously parted the waters of the Jordan—at flood level (see Joshua 3:15–16)—so they could safely cross with the ark of the covenant, housing the Ten Commandments. To mark the location, they gathered twelve large stones, one for each tribe of Israel. The display would serve as "a memorial to the people of Israel forever" (see Joshua 4:6–7).

This place was named Gilgal, however, because of another major event occurring there not long after the Israelites had crossed the Jordan. After God delivered them from Egypt, the Israelites wandered for forty years before reaching the Promised Land. By then, the younger generations of men were no longer being circumcised. But God had established circumcision as a powerful symbolic act of the covenant He established with His people, beginning with Abraham and the men of his household (see Genesis 17:10–14). So before they could take possession of the land, God told Joshua, their leader, "Make flint knives and circumcise the Israelites again" (Joshua 5:2).

Afterward, God declared, "Today I have rolled away the reproach of Egypt from you," which apparently is why the place came to be called Gilgal (Joshua 5:9). In Hebrew, the word for "roll" is similar to "Gilgal," both as a verb as well as a noun. Thus, the name refers to the circle of stones the Israelites had gathered, which were likely so large they had to be rolled into formation, as well as this explanatory message the Lord provided to Joshua about rolling away "the reproach of Egypt."

Your Gilgal likely represents a place of rolling as well, a threshold where you encountered God's grace in powerful ways. At this place, whether a literal location or a symbolic spot, you cut ties with old habits, addictions and default patterns of behavior. You recognized all God had done to help you move beyond your past. Remembering your Gilgal remains a powerful way to celebrate where you are and to anticipate where God is leading you!

Today, spend a few moments prayerfully reflecting on your own personal Gilgal.

For in Christ Jesus neither circumcision nor uncircumcision has any value. The only thing that counts is faith expressing itself through love.

Galatians 5:6

· · · · ·

Lord, just as You did for the people of Israel, You have often parted the floodwaters around me and made a way for me to go through them. When I have fallen, You have forgiven my sins and given me a fresh anointing of Your grace. Thank You for always picking me up and leading the way. Amen.

DAY 33

At Gilgal, you are completely separated from the old you, from the broken you, from the sinful you, from the defeated you. God is now telling you there's nothing in your past that can stop your anointed future.

Gilgal was the place where all the men who came into the Promised Land were circumcised in order to separate them from their past. Implicitly, Gilgal offered an important message to these younger generations: "Your parents didn't make it, but you will." While their parents had disobeyed and rebelled against God, and therefore were not allowed to enter the Promised Land, these newly circumcised men were getting another chance, a fresh start. By requiring their circumcision, God indicated that they were once again being set apart from the reproach of the past. They were now accomplishing what their ancestors did not accomplish.

We all need a place like Gilgal on our journey of faith. Gilgal is God's way of allowing us to come clean before Him and start anew. It's as if the calendar has been reset to start a new year, a fresh beginning, a reboot of the spiritual system we've been running in the hard drive of our soul. When we establish and claim Gilgal in our lives, we're not only creating an altar to praise and thank God for getting us to this point, but also being reminded that God has completely separated us from who we used to be. We are no longer covered by the reproach, shame, guilt, fear and punishment of the past. Instead, we discover God's grace at our own personal Gilgal, a crossroads for the cross of Christ in our lives.

At Gilgal, you are completely separated from the old you, from the broken you, from the sinful you, from the defeated you. God is now telling you there is nothing in your past that can stop your anointed future.

> You're no longer the liar you once were.
> You're no longer the thief you once were.
> You're no longer the cheater you once were.
> You're no longer the gossip you once were.
> You're no longer the fornicator you once were.
> You're no longer the adulterer you once were.
> You're no longer the coveter you once were.
> You're no longer the murderer you once were.
> You're no longer the self-righteous legalist you once were.
> You are a new creature, washed clean from all the iniquities of your past by the blood of the Lamb, Jesus Christ!

As you transition from pushing your plow of perseverance to wearing your mantle of promotion, God will lead you to Gilgal before you continue your journey. There, He reminds you that you have been reborn, changed, set apart. At Gilgal, God reminds you that the pain of your past can never compare to the prize of your future. Gilgal changes everything!

> **Rejoice today in the knowledge that who you used to be is not who you are now!**

Therefore, if anyone is in Christ, the new creation has come: The old has gone, the new is here!

2 Corinthians 5:17

. . . . .

Father God, I'm overwhelmed by Your loving mercy and life-changing grace. Praise be to You for sending Your Son, Jesus, so that I can live free from sin and death! Thank You for transforming me into His image day by day. Amen.

DAY
34

If you want to experience all that God has for you, it is time to grow up. Gilgal marks the place where you are weaned from milk and mature enough to eat spiritual meat.

Perhaps you have stopped at one of those welcome centers, tourist bureaus or visitors' rest areas as you cross from one state to the next or from one country to another. Residents want you to acknowledge that you are no longer where you were but on their turf now. These places mark the transition from one locale to another.

Gilgal marked a similar significant transition for the Israelites. After they had crossed the Jordan and rolled twelve stones together to form an eternal monument, after they had obeyed the Lord's instructions and been circumcised, the Israelites stayed at Gilgal long enough to heal and to celebrate Passover. This celebration also marked another turning point: "The day after the Passover, that very day, they ate some of the produce of the land: unleavened bread and roasted grain. The manna stopped the day after they ate this food from the land; there was no longer any manna for the Israelites, but that year they ate the produce of Canaan" (Joshua 5:11–12).

During their forty years in the wilderness, the Israelites ate manna, similar to unleavened bread, which the Lord provided daily. Manna could not be collected and saved for later; each day's supply was intended to nourish people in the present only. Having finally reached Canaan, the long-awaited land flowing with milk and honey, the people were crossing into a new place of maturity. God no longer provided manna for them because they had arrived!

God's people had matured enough to trust Him because of His faithfulness. The Lord had taken care of them each step of the way, despite their rebellion, idolatry and bitter complaints. Now the Almighty had made good on His promise and brought them to the Promised Land of Canaan. And in many ways, Gilgal was like the welcome station created to commemorate such a monumental milestone. It wasn't their final destination, but merely a place to catch their physical, emotional and spiritual bearings before exploring their new home.

Think of your Gilgal in the same way—a kind of spiritual welcome center for the new life awaiting you. You're not where you used to be! You have matured and grown and developed spiritually so that you no longer need milk but are finally ready for meat. With maturity comes the transition from your plow to your mantle, which includes new responsibilities. God's expectations are clear: "You have been believers so long now that you ought to be teaching others" rather than needing "someone to teach you again the basic things about God's word" (Hebrews 5:12 NLT).

If you want to experience all that God has for you, then it's time to grow up!

Anyone who lives on milk, being still an infant, is not acquainted with the teaching about righteousness. But solid food is for the mature, who by constant use have trained themselves to distinguish good from evil.

Hebrews 5:13–14

. . . . .

Lord, I have learned so much, and I want to learn so much more. But I also accept the responsibilities that come with wearing Your mantle of prophetic power. Nourish me with the solid food of Your Holy Spirit so that I may nourish others with Your love. Amen.

DAY 35

As we transition into wearing our mantle of promotion, we often find that a quick glimpse of Gilgal fortifies us with faith for where the Lord will lead us next. Such visits remind us that we are no longer residents of our past, but citizens of a glorious, heavenly future!

Elijah was about to cross over from earth into heaven, and returning to Gilgal, he honored its sacred history. There, he recalled what God had done not only for the people of Israel historically but also for Elijah personally. In between outracing Ahab's chariot in the rainstorm by tucking and running (see 1 Kings 18:45–46) and finding Elisha in the field plowing (see 1 Kings 19:19), Elijah spiraled to his lowest point. Afraid, he ran for his life, left his servant in Beersheba and journeyed into the wilderness alone. Eventually, Elijah stopped under a broom bush and prayed that he might die (see 1 Kings 19:5).

You can probably relate. We all experience times when we feel as though we can't go on, like we're at the end of our rope. We feel exhausted, overwhelmed, depleted and discouraged. Our mantle feels too heavy to wear, and we can't muster the energy to keep going.

God didn't abandon Elijah, but He met him where he was. After providing rest and nourishment for the prophet's body, God instructed Elijah to meet Him on Mount Horeb, where the Lord displayed His limitless power through the natural world. While Elijah watched from his cave, God reminded the prophet whom he served—almighty God, Creator of heaven and earth! And rather than telling Elijah not to feel depressed and hopeless, the Lord gave him a mission—to find Elisha and mentor him as he took up his own mantle.

Remembering our purpose continues to be one of the best, most effective cures whenever we're struggling. Our enemy likes to use those opportunities in the hope we will feel sorry for ourselves and give in to temptation. But when we take our focus off ourselves and our feelings, we rediscover the joy that comes from serving others. We discover the maturity that comes with wearing the mantle.

Which brings us full circle back to Gilgal. After enduring such an excruciating season of depression, Elijah went on to train Elisha and prepare him for the time when he would be on his own. So, as they anticipated God taking Elijah to heaven, they made one last holy pilgrimage together. It had been a curving, crazy road to get there, but because they were following God, they knew it was worthwhile.

You know this truth as well. Rarely does God lead you in a straight, predictable route based on human logic. Instead, He guides you through deserts and droughts, through fire and rain, through moments of darkness when you feel lost and alone. And then, God meets you right where you are and empowers you with a fresh encounter with His Spirit!

Let your Gilgal be the vantage point for looking ahead at where God wants to lead you next!

But the Advocate, the Holy Spirit, whom the Father will send in my name, will teach you all things and will remind you of everything I have said to you.

John 14:26

· · · · ·

Heavenly Father, thank You for the many ways You have sustained me, nourished me and empowered me, especially when I felt like I could not go on. May I never become so focused on my emotions that I lose sight of You and Your unconditional love. I can't wait to see where You will lead me next! Amen.

DAY
36

You will never leave your plow behind and
be ready to accept the mantle of promotion if
you don't keep your eyes on the prize.

Each day you encounter countless options vying for your attention, pulling you away from your path of prophetic power. But you will never leave your plow behind and be ready to accept the mantle of promotion if you don't keep your eyes on the prize. Learning to discipline your focus requires always keeping your eyes on Jesus.

Even the most passionate, dedicated believers can be pulled in too many directions as distractions divert their attention and dilute their energy. We live in an age when we are told we can have everything, try everything and be whoever we want, whenever we want. But this is simply not true! God created us in His own holy image, and He knows us better than we know ourselves. Only a relationship with Him can ever satisfy our deepest core longings for love, intimacy and purpose.

That is why the enemy of our souls works so hard to distract us and prevent us from focusing on what is true, what is real, what is eternal. If we can be conned into thinking that we can control our lives, we won't rely on God's power and trust His guidance on a daily basis. We can have a compartmentalized faith of distance and detachment, but it pales compared to enjoying the passionate relationship we can have with the Spirit of the living God dwelling in us.

During his season of depression, Elijah allowed the queen's death threats to get in his head. He allowed his own exhaustion to overwhelm his thoughts and emotions. He wandered into the wilderness alone and away from God. But the Lord refused to give up on Elijah and met him in the depths of the prophet's despair. God provided for his needs before giving him a new mission. Elijah began to see clearly again and envisioned a new future, one determined by obeying God and fulfilling His purpose.

As you follow Elijah's example and move into your mantle of promotion, keep your vision focused—not on yourself, your feelings, your circumstances—but on following God's direction for your life. To move forward in your God-given purpose and grow in your faith, you must focus exclusively on Jesus. Continue to immerse yourself in God's Word and become attuned to the voice of the Holy Spirit. All priorities must begin and end with your relationship with the heavenly Father. Jesus is your Role Model, the Author and Perfecter of your faith. If you want to overcome the many detours, distractions and diversions of the enemy, it's time to lock your eyes on the Lord!

**Today, remember your first love
and stay focused on Jesus!**

Set your minds on things above, not on earthly things.

Colossians 3:2

. . . . .

Father, I am so easily distracted at times, allowing my mind and heart to stray from You and the path You have set for me. Give me strength and stamina, wisdom and discernment so that I may remain fixed on knowing You, loving You and serving others for Your glory. Amen.

DAY
37

Traveling from Gilgal to Bethel, Elijah and Elisha
symbolically bridged the past and the future.
Similarly, when you leave Gilgal behind, the pain of
your past becomes the hope for a better future.

T he secret to keeping your eyes on the prize is looking ahead and not behind.

If Gilgal is about recognizing and honoring the hard places in your life, then the next stop on Elijah's farewell tour, Bethel, reminds you to hold on to your dreams. Once you have taken on your mantle of power and promotion, you must remain faithful to the course God has revealed to you. God's promises will be fulfilled as you bring your divinely inspired dreams to life.

Bethel, which means "house of God," was named by Jacob, who himself later received a new name from God, Israel. While his journey to becoming the father of a nation was never easy, Jacob experienced the life-transforming power of God through a special dream at what would become a special place. After cheating his twin brother, Esau, out of his birthright, Jacob tricked their father, Isaac, into blessing him with what was rightfully not Jacob's to receive (see Genesis 27). Furious over the deception, Esau vowed to kill his brother, which prompted their mother, Rebekah, to send Jacob on the road to stay with her brother, Laban, in Haran until Esau cooled down (see Genesis 27:42–43).

So there was Jacob, escaping from the wrath of his family, when God shared a dream of his divine destiny. While sleeping, Jacob dreamed of stairs reaching from earth to heaven, with angels going up and down its steps. At the top stood God, who told Jacob that he would become the father of a nation with countless descendants (see Genesis 28:13–14). Then the Lord blessed him: "I am with you and will watch over you wherever you go, and I will bring you back to this land. I will not leave you until I have done what I have promised you" (Genesis 28:15).

No matter how badly Jacob had blown it back home, or how terribly he would blow it again, he had a God-given dream to realize. Jacob knew he could let go of his past because God had revealed his future. Climbing the ladder to his dreams would make stretching for each rung worth it.

Traveling from Gilgal to Bethel, the name Jacob had given to his anointed dream site, Elijah and Elisha symbolically bridged the past and the future. Just as Jacob watched the movie trailer for the epic legacy he would leave, Elijah ventured to Bethel knowing he was about to go to his ultimate destination, his heavenly home with God. His journey to Bethel, along with Jacob's dream there, reminds us that we, too, are in between the struggles of the past and the dream of the future.

> **Just like Jacob, and just like Elijah, you are about to see what you have never seen before!**

Brothers and sisters, I do not consider myself yet to have taken hold of it. But one thing I do: Forgetting what is behind and straining toward what is ahead, I press on toward the goal to win the prize for which God has called me heavenward in Christ Jesus.

Philippians 3:13–14

· · · · ·

Lord, thank You for planting Your dream inside me and blessing me with Your mantle of power and promotion. Help me to look forward and not behind as I focus on fulfilling the divine destiny that You have designed uniquely for me. Amen.

DAY
38

When you reach a Bethel milestone, God will
fulfill your dreams and give you more dreams.

When you were living in your past, you didn't have a dream—only an illusion. Running in place, stuck on a treadmill of your own making, you were not plowing with perseverance, but rather digging a rut that only grew deeper the more you relied on your own power rather than on God's. But at Bethel, your nightmare is replaced with God's dream for your life.

Once the heavenly ladder of your dreams appears before you, it changes your life. Because you're no longer where you used to be—you are on your way up! You and your family can now glimpse heaven coming down. When God gives you His dream for your life, nothing can stop you from ascending toward higher places. Your climb probably will not be easy, but it will lead to things you have never seen before or even imagined.

Others may treat you differently because dreamers are dangerous. Jacob, the founder of Bethel, discovered this as he dealt with his brother, his uncle, his wives and his children. Joseph, who was Jacob's youngest and favorite son, learned the hard way that your dreams can make others jealous.

But when you faithfully steward all that God gives you, your dreams can also save you. Joseph was summoned from prison, where he landed after being falsely accused by Potiphar's wife, to interpret Pharaoh's dreams. Because of Joseph's gifts as a dreamer, he not only explained what Pharaoh's dreams meant, but he became second-in-command of all of Egypt.

Another Joseph was also a dreamer, a carpenter from Nazareth engaged to a young virgin named Mary. When she was chosen to be the mother of Jesus, Joseph planned to do the honorable thing and discreetly call off their engagement. But he received a message from God in a dream that instructed him to honor his pledge to Mary and to proceed with their marriage, which he did. Later, after Mary had given birth to Christ in a stable in Bethlehem, Joseph was warned in a dream to flee to Egypt to escape danger from King Herod.

God has always used dreams and dreamers to accomplish His purposes—and He still does! His Word tells us, "In the last days, God says, I will pour out my Spirit on all people. Your sons and daughters will prophesy, your young men will see visions, your old men will dream dreams" (Acts 2:17). This promise reminds us that we dream not only for ourselves but also for our children, for our children's children, for our community and for our nation.

As God fulfills your dreams, you will discover new ones carrying you into His glorious future!

Commit your work to the LORD, and your plans will be established.

Proverbs 16:3 ESV

· · · · ·

Dear God, You give me dreams that can only be fulfilled when I trust You and step out in faith. Grant me the courage to risk my comfort and safety in order to accomplish the impossible for Your glory. Amen.

DAY
39

Don't get lost on the road between Gilgal and
Bethel and end up stuck in place. Instead, keep
dreaming and hoping and trusting God each day.

As you transition from your plow to your mantle, your maturity and commitment will likely be tested at some point. You may be tempted to focus on the perks of your privilege rather than the diligence and dedication that got you there. If you're not careful, you may get stuck in between where you were and where you are going.

Elijah likely worried that his successor, Elisha, might fall into such a trap. At each stop of his farewell tour, Elijah kept telling Elisha to "stay here" before setting off for the next location, while each time Elisha insisted, "I will not leave you" (2 Kings 2:1–8). Elijah perhaps wanted to prepare his apprentice for the imminent time when they would no longer be together, grooming Elisha to take the full weight of the mantle as God's prophet. Elisha, however, refused to abandon Elijah, even for a seemingly logical reason, because of his commitment to his mentor and to the Lord.

When Elijah told Elisha to stay, he was also testing his successor. Although God had led Elijah to this young man in the fields, the prophet perhaps wanted one last confirmation of Elisha's dedication to the job. If Elisha remained committed to Elijah, then the younger prophet would remain committed to God after Elijah departed for heaven.

Elisha could have chosen to obey his teacher and remain home. But Elisha had matured enough to say, "No! Wherever you go, I will go." When others protect us or sacrifice for us, it's easy to convince ourselves we can stay put. But as believers, as children of the cross, as those designated to live life abundantly, we must continue moving forward from good to great. When you linger in between, you get stuck.

Stuck in good when God has something great.

Stuck surviving when God wants you thriving.

Stuck in the status quo when God wants to shake things up.

No matter how good it seems, to stay there when God calls you forward is a step backward. The Lord has more for you! Trust Him that the dream weavers in your life are there to accompany you on your spiritual journey. This is not the time to be satisfied with being sidelined.

The only way to resist settling is to keep your eyes on the prize. You must stay focused and want more—more of God in every area of your life. And when you have your eyes on the eternal prize, you should be prepared to swim in an overflowing tide of blessings. Because when you wear the mantle of promotion and commit to going the distance, you will receive more than you can ever imagine!

> **Today, don't settle for less than God's best for your life!**

From everyone who has been given much, much will be demanded; and from the one who has been entrusted with much, much more will be asked.

Luke 12:48

. . . . .

Dear God, when things are going well in my life, I am often tempted to stay even when You prompt me to go. Give me the courage to always step out in faith no matter how good my circumstances may be. Help me trust You for the great things ahead! Amen.

DAY 40

When you keep your eyes on the prize, your hard place will become your high place. Wearing the mantle of promotion, you discover that failure is not an option!

Once you invite Jesus into your life and His Spirit into your heart, failure is not an option. You are not a failure, and you were never a failure—you are God's beloved child, washed by the blood of the Lamb, forgiven and made new. Not only are you not a failure, but you will never live in failure. And not only are you not a failure and not only will you never live in failure again, but all those who follow behind you will never be failures or live in failure!

When you are in God's hands, how can you live in failure? His Word promises us, "From eternity to eternity I am God. No one can snatch anyone out of my hand. No one can undo what I have done" (Isaiah 43:13 NLT). We are assured by Jesus, "I give them eternal life, and they shall never perish; no one will snatch them out of my hand" (John 10:28).

Even when we fall, we fall within the confines of the shadow of the Almighty.

We fall in grace and in the hand of God.

Falling is not failure when you are in the hands of God!

Elijah knew firsthand that his falling was not his failure, a truth he then passed on to Elisha. Elijah had seen God do astounding, amazing, awe-inspiring miracles, and yet the prophet still got scared, still ran away, still hid in a cave. Even there, in the darkness of Elijah's fear, exhaustion, anxiety and despair,

God met him. God still provided for him and restored not only Elijah's body, but his spirit.

Elijah knew what it meant to be a soul survivor, and so do you.

How did you survive? Because the Lord was with you! He said, "When you go through deep waters, I will be with you. When you go through rivers of difficulty, you will not drown. When you walk through the fire of oppression, you will not be burned up; the flames will not consume you" (Isaiah 43:2 NLT).

When you have survived life's trials and tribulations, when you have suffered unexpected losses and battled illness, when you have been through addiction and broken relationships, when you have come through all the abuse, betrayal and neglect others have thrown at you, then you know that failure is not an option. Your eyes are on the prize, and God's power makes you unstoppable. You may be forced to slow down, take a detour, stop to catch your breath or seek a new direction. But you cannot be stopped, any more than Elisha could be stopped from accompanying Elijah in his final days.

> **Survivors know that as they mature in their faith, they become thrivers.**

So we are convinced that every detail of our lives is continually woven together to fit into God's perfect plan of bringing good into our lives, for we are his lovers who have been called to fulfill his designed purpose.

Romans 8:28 TPT

. . . . .

Father God, You have brought me through so much and never given up on me! Thank You for sustaining me with the power of Your Spirit when I could not go on. I praise You for the gift of salvation through Your Son, Jesus Christ. I am a soul survivor, Your trophy of grace! Amen.

DAY
41

In order to step into the promise of God, we must remove
every encumbrance, even as we bow before Him.

When you're living in the promise, it can be challenging, frustrating or overwhelming to wait for its fulfillment. But as you experience the prophetic power that comes with your mantle of promotion, your discovery leads to the next step and then the next. As God reveals His presence, overcomes all obstacles and creates a way where you cannot see one, you begin to trust Him more and more.

This is the message emerging from Elijah's third stop on his farewell tour before being swept up to heaven in a chariot of fire. After leaving Gilgal to go to Bethel, Elijah then headed to Jericho. Just as Gilgal and Bethel held significant spiritual history, Jericho did as well.

After Joshua, led by the Lord, shepherded the people of Israel into Canaan, Jericho was the first city standing between them and claiming the Promised Land. They had escaped Egypt by running through the Red Sea, which parted miraculously for their passage; they wandered in the wilderness for forty years; they crossed the Jordan River, which also parted for them; and now they had finally arrived at their divine destination only to hit a wall, literally—the defensive wall protecting the city of Jericho.

Despite God's promises kept to them, the Israelites wondered how they could possibly conquer a fortified city like

Jericho. Prior to entering Canaan, Moses and Aaron had sent out spies, including Joshua and eleven others, for a reconnaissance report—and the news wasn't good. When they returned, ten of the spies thought they could *never* overtake the Canaanites, comparing themselves to grasshoppers in their midst (see Numbers 13:33). Only Joshua and Caleb had faith that the Lord would fulfill His promise and empower them to win this land.

When you wear your divine mantle of promotion, you can rest assured that God's limitless power is more than enough to take down any wall you encounter. No matter how high, wide, strong or well-guarded it may be, no wall can withstand the supernatural power of almighty God! It may not fall exactly the way you think it will or when you think it will, but it will fall in God's perfect timing.

When your resources are depleted, God provides all you need. When life throws you a curve ball, God empowers you to hit it out of the park. When you see no way forward, God opens a path.

> **Today, refuse to fear any walls you encounter—trust God to make a bridge!**

Ah, Sovereign LORD, you have made the heavens and the earth by your great power and outstretched arm. Nothing is too hard for you.

Jeremiah 32:17

· · · · ·

Dear Lord, when I encounter walls that block the path You have chosen for me, I know You will make a way. What seems impossible to me is always possible for You. May I trust You completely, no matter how high those walls may be! Amen.

DAY
42

No matter what struggle you're facing, the Lord always reveals a way forward—just as Rahab experienced when the people of Israel were about to conquer her city.

When you boldly risk trusting God in all areas of your life, you experience deliverance even in overwhelming circumstances. Jericho was not only well known to Elijah and Elisha as the place where God brought the city walls down so His people could enter the Promised Land—Jericho was also home to Rahab, a woman known to be a prostitute in the city, as well as a risk-taker for God.

When two of Joshua's spies came knocking on her door while scouting out the city, Rahab agreed to hide them from the king's men in exchange for the safety of her family when the Israelites later attacked the city. She had heard of the Lord's power in rescuing the Israelites from Egypt and sustaining them until they reached Canaan (see Joshua 2). Although she knew very little about their God, Rahab trusted that He was the only One who could save her in the dire situation about to unfold. Logically, she had no reason to trust the foreign spies she was willing to harbor at great risk to the very family she wanted to save. But the Spirit of God must have gently whispered to her heart to take a giant leap of faith.

Rahab reminds us that God uses anyone willing to trust Him. Rahab was a Canaanite, automatically the enemy of the Israelites, as well as a prostitute, someone who earned a living by doing what the Lord had commanded the Israelites to reserve exclusively for marriage between one man and one woman. Her great act of faith was to lie to her own countrymen, basically committing an act of treason.

Yet Rahab—arguably the least likely to serve God boldly, at least on paper—is included in the "faith hall of fame" recounted in Hebrews: "By faith the prostitute Rahab, because she welcomed the spies, was not killed with those who were disobedient" (Hebrews 11:31). By trusting God, Rahab experienced the fulfillment of a promise made to spare her life. Consequently, she discovered a new life beyond her wildest dreams—and a role as an ancestor of Jesus Christ.

The longer you wear your mantle of promotion, the more you may be required to trust God, not only to bring down enormous walls, but with risks that force you to choose your allegiance. When political parties and social causes compete for your support, remember that only the Lord should have your wholehearted devotion. The cause of Christ always comes first!

> ### Step out in faith with a bold trust in God's ability to save you!

But if serving the LORD seems undesirable to you, then choose for yourselves this day whom you will serve. . . . But as for me and my household, we will serve the LORD.

Joshua 24:15

· · · · ·

Lord, when others try to divide my loyalties, strengthen my resolve to serve and obey You above all. Just as Rahab trusted You for her deliverance despite human logic, may I boldly step out in faith and trust You to reveal my way. Amen.

DAY
43

The Jericho promise is fundamental to your
plow of perseverance and prophetic mantle of
promotion. It's a holy shout-out to those who stand
in your way that God is bringing them down. It's
the heavenly trumpet blast celebrating the Jericho
that God has already delivered in your life!

While Joshua had seen God do the impossible many times already, he might still have wondered exactly how God would bring down the walls of Jericho. As it turned out, the Lord used Jericho to convey an important lesson to His people about finding their voice. Rather than utilize military might to bring down its walls, God instructed them to shout them down:

> "See, I have delivered Jericho into your hands, along with its king and its fighting men. March around the city once with all the armed men. Do this for six days. Have seven priests carry trumpets of rams' horns in front of the ark. On the seventh day, march around the city seven times, with the priests blowing the trumpets. When you hear them sound a long blast on the trumpets, have the whole army give a loud shout; then the wall of the city will collapse and the army will go up, everyone straight in."
>
> Joshua 6:2–5

Notice the Lord told Joshua that He had already delivered Jericho, including its king and army, into the Israelites' hands. Yes, that's *delivered*—past tense! God has already won the victory for us as well.

Whatever your Jericho might be, the Lord has already delivered it into your hands, and now you must shout down its walls and claim His promise.

No matter what it is, the Lord has already won the battle for you—just like He won for the people of Israel when they did as He instructed:

On the seventh day, they got up at daybreak and marched around the city seven times in the same manner, except that on that day they circled the city seven times. The seventh time around, when the priests sounded the trumpet blast, Joshua commanded the army, "Shout! For the LORD has given you the city!"

Joshua 6:15–16

Finding your voice and shouting out in obedience to the Lord remains a resounding theme in Jericho. The taking of Jericho is yet another classic underdog story. And while it inspires anyone facing seemingly insurmountable odds, the Jericho promise holds true for all of us.

What is the Jericho promise? It's the power of God to transform every wall we face into a bridge to a glorious future! It's the promise that the walls blocking your progress into the future God has for you are about to come tumbling down. It's the holy shout rumbling from your mouth until your throat is sore and your voice is hoarse. The Jericho promise is your expectation of God's power to make a way where you cannot—and the anticipation of what's waiting on the other side of your walls!

Today, claim the Jericho promise and watch the Lord bring down your walls!

Shout joyfully to the LORD, all the earth; Break forth and sing for joy and sing praises.

Psalm 98:4 NASB1995

·　·　·　·　·

God of heaven and earth, thank You for the ways I see Your Jericho promise being fulfilled in my life. Through Your power, all my walls are coming down! Amen.

DAY 44

If we want our walls to become a bridge for future generations, then we must shout those walls down, removing anything that separates us from where we are and where God wants us to be.

t was no accident that Elijah, along with Elisha, visited Jericho on his farewell-to-earth tour because, like the other stops on his route, Jericho represents a timeless truth about who God is and how He loves us. If you want to see what you have never seen before, then you must claim the promises of God and believe in their ongoing fulfillment. You must persevere, no matter how large the problem or how impossible the deficit.

In other words, do not be dismayed, baffled, perplexed or shaken when a wall appears in your journey! Why? Because, simply stated, there's a promise behind that wall! There's an opportunity behind that obstacle! There's God's favor behind your fear!

Wherever you are in your journey, the wall ahead cannot stop you.

That wall will become your bridge by the power of the living God!

The same Lord of heaven and earth who empowered the shouts of His people to bring down the walls of Jericho will empower you to do the same for the walls in your life!

You must shout down the walls separating where you are from where God wants you to be. You must shout down the adversaries and the obstacles blocking your path. You must obliterate your walls so that one day your children will climb over the rubble and give God thanks and praise for what He did through you. They will survey the ruins and get tears in their eyes, recognizing and celebrating the fact that someone—their mother, father, grandmother, grandfather, brother, sister, aunt, uncle—loved them enough to bring down the walls so that they would not be incarcerated by them. They will have their own walls to bring down, but they will not have to deal with the walls God allowed you to shout into crumbling ruins.

When you live in the Jericho promise of God's power to persevere, keep marching until it's time to shout. When you're pushing your plow and don't know how you will go on, keep pushing until it's time to shout. When you're wearing your mantle of promotion and come up against obstacles bigger than the ones before, keep pushing and praying and persevering until it's time to shout. And when God says it's time to shout, then SHOUT like you mean it!

When you confront a trial, a temptation, a trauma or a tempest, you know what to do. You must be willing by faith in Jesus Christ to go around it, praise it down with your shouts and then climb over it. You march, then you praise, then you climb! You walk, you worship and you win!

> Today, get ready to shout down the walls that are holding you back from all God has for you!

I waited patiently for the LORD; he turned to me and heard my cry.

Psalm 40:1

．．．．．

God, grant me patience to wait on Your timing, and then by Your power, to shout down every wall in my way. May every wall that comes down in my life be for Your glory! Amen.

DAY 45

When you can't see a way forward, God is the
Waymaker! If you want the power to persevere to
promotion, then follow the Waymaker and watch
walls crumble and bridges take their place.

n Jericho, surely Elijah and Elisha could hear the echoes of those shouts from Joshua and the Israelites so many generations before, if not audibly then spiritually. And their visit there must have been bittersweet because after Jericho, it was time for their final destination before the Lord swept Elijah up to heaven: Jordan.

When they reached this last stop, Elijah used his Jericho promise to make a Jordan discovery. Having lived a lifetime of watching God do the impossible again and again, Elijah likely wasn't fazed by the issue of how to cross the Jordan River. The prophet did what came naturally by this time in his life—*super*naturally: "Elijah took his cloak, rolled it up and struck the water with it. The water divided to the right and to the left, and the two of them crossed over on dry ground" (2 Kings 2:8).

His cloak represented divine authority, his calling, his anointing, his gift from God. So in their final moments together, Elijah didn't talk to Elisha about how the cloak worked—he *showed* him. Through his actions, Elijah silently communicated, *Okay, pay attention. I'm going to show you what to do whenever you find yourself in front of a circumstance where there is no way to get across. You take the anointing, the authority, the gift, the grace, that God has given you and exercise it. Watch carefully because this is how it's done!*

Before Elijah departed, he left his heir the greatest gift he had to give. He showed him one powerful truth: *Our God is the Waymaker!*

We need a generation of leaders who will show the emerging generation how to do it! People who say, "I'm not going to tell you how to live in victory; I'm going to show you what it is to live in victory. I'm not just going to tell you how to overcome; I'm going to show you how to overcome."

Now is the time for you to step up and demonstrate the power of your mantle without saying a word. *Watch me move that mountain. Watch me kick that devil out. Watch me shout down walls. Watch me pray down the fire. Watch me prophesy the rain. Watch me tuck my mantle and run faster than chariots.*

You must live in the power of the Jordan discovery, just as Elisha did.

God will make a way where there is no way!

He will make a way when all the doors close in your face.

He will make a way when your detractors say, "No way!"

He will make a way when hell says, "NO way!

He will make a way even when *you* say, "NO WAY!"

> **If you want the power to persevere to promotion, then follow the Waymaker!**

For I am about to do something new. See, I have already begun! Do you not see it? I will make a pathway through the wilderness. I will create rivers in the dry wasteland.

Isaiah 43:19 NLT

· · · · ·

Heavenly Father, You are my Waymaker, and I praise Your holy name! Thank You for my mantle of promotion and the power to persevere. I can do all things through Christ, who strengthens me! Amen.

Samuel Rodriguez is president of the National Hispanic Christian Leadership Conference (NHCLC), the world's largest Hispanic Christian organization, with more than 42,000 U.S. churches and many additional churches spread throughout the Spanish-speaking diaspora.

Rodriguez stands recognized by CNN, Fox News, Univision and Telemundo as America's most influential Latino/Hispanic faith leader. *Charisma* magazine named him one of the forty leaders who changed the world. The *Wall Street Journal* named him one of the top-twelve Latino leaders, and he was the only faith leader on that list. He has been named among the "Top 100 Christian Leaders in America" (Newsmax 2018) and nominated as one of the "100 Most Influential People in the World" (*Time* 2013). Rodriguez is regularly featured on CNN, Fox News, Univision, PBS, *Christianity Today*, the *New York Times*, the *Wall Street Journal* and many others.

Rodriguez was the first Latino to deliver the keynote address at the annual Martin Luther King Jr. Commemorative Service at Ebenezer Baptist Church, and he is a recipient of the Martin Luther King Jr. Leadership Award presented by the Congress of Racial Equality.

Rodriguez advised former American presidents Bush, Obama and Trump, and he frequently consults with Congress advancing immigration and criminal justice reform as well as religious freedom and pro-life initiatives. By the grace of God, the Rev. Samuel Rodriguez is one of the few individuals—and the first Latino evangelical—to have participated in the inauguration ceremonies of two different presidents representing both political parties.

Rodriguez is the executive producer of two films: *Breakthrough*, the GMA Dove Award winner for Inspirational Film of the Year, with an Academy Award nomination for Best Original Song, and *Flamin' Hot*, in partnership with Franklin Entertainment and 20th Century Fox. He is also co-founder of TBN Salsa, an international Christian-based broadcast television network, and he is the author of *You Are Next, Shake Free, Be Light*—a number-one *L.A. Times* bestseller—and *From Survive to Thrive*, a number-one Amazon bestseller.

He earned his master's degree from Lehigh University and has received honorary doctorates from Northwest, William Jessup and Baptist University of the Americas.

Rodriguez serves as the senior pastor of New Season Church, one of America's fastest-growing megachurches and number thirteen on Newsmax's Top 50 megachurches in America, with campuses in Los Angeles and Sacramento, California, where he resides with his wife, Eva, and their three children.

For more information, please visit

www.PastorSam.com

RevSamuelRodriguez

@pastorsamuelrodriguez

@nhclc